T0318998

Cambridge Elements ☰

Elements in Business Strategy
edited by
J.-C. Spender
Rutgers Business School

CORPORATE SOCIAL RESPONSIBILITY

Christopher Wickert
Vrije Universiteit Amsterdam (VU), The Netherlands

David Risi
University of St. Gallen, Switzerland

CAMBRIDGE
UNIVERSITY PRESS

CAMBRIDGE
UNIVERSITY PRESS

University Printing House, Cambridge CB2 8BS, United Kingdom

One Liberty Plaza, 20th Floor, New York, NY 10006, USA

477 Williamstown Road, Port Melbourne, VIC 3207, Australia

314–321, 3rd Floor, Plot 3, Splendor Forum, Jasola District Centre,
New Delhi – 110025, India

79 Anson Road, #06–04/06, Singapore 079906

Cambridge University Press is part of the University of Cambridge.

It furthers the University's mission by disseminating knowledge in the pursuit of education, learning, and research at the highest international levels of excellence.

www.cambridge.org
Information on this title: www.cambridge.org/9781108745260
DOI: 10.1017/9781108775298

First published 2019

A catalogue record for this publication is available from the British Library.

ISBN 978-1-108-74526-0 Paperback
ISSN 2515-0693 (online)
ISSN 2515-0685 (print)

Corporate Social Responsibility

Elements in Business Strategy

DOI: 10.1017/9781108775298
First published online: July 2019

Christopher Wickert
Vrije Universiteit Amsterdam

David Risi
University of St. Gallen

Author for correspondence: Christopher Wickert, christopher.wickert@vu.nl

Abstract: This Element offers a thought-provoking and critical examination of Corporate Social Responsibility (CSR). CSR has entered the boardroom and become a mainstream management concept for businesses to address their ethical, social and environmental responsibilities towards society. CSR does not come without contestation, and firms engage in CSR for different reasons and exhibit different patterns of CSR activities. These activities range from sincere action with substantial social or environmental improvements to symbolic impression management and the creation of a CSR facade that is little more than empty words. This Element illuminates and scrutinizes contemporary approaches to CSR and offers a fresh perspective for scholars, managers and decision-makers interested in the societal role of business firms beyond maximizing profitability. Christopher Wickert and David Risi take a step back from how CSR is currently understood and practised, and encourage readers to reflect on how to move CSR forward towards a more inclusive concept.

Keywords: Business Ethics; Corporate Social Responsibility (CSR); Corporate Social Irresponsibility (CSiR); Digitalization; Implementation; Globalization; Greenwashing; Social Connection; Sustainable Development Goals (SDGs); United Nations Global Compact

ISBNs:9781108745260 (PB), 9781108775298 (OC)
ISSNs: 2515-0693 (online), 2515-0685 (print)

Contents

Introduction

Corporate Social Responsibility (CSR) is a contested phenomenon. Here, we refer to CSR as an umbrella term to describe how business firms, small and large, integrate social, environmental and ethical responsibilities to which they are connected into their core business strategies, structures and procedures within and across divisions, functions as well as value chains in collaboration with relevant stakeholders. As yet, there is no consensus as to what exactly these responsibilities are, how to best address them, and more generally what the role of business in society is and should be. Researchers, managers, politicians and other stakeholders such as the media have not reached an agreement about the scope and content of CSR. At the same time, CSR has moved from the margins to the mainstream. It now takes centre stage in managerial and scholarly discourses and has entered the boardroom of most corporations.

Our aim with this Element is to shed light on the contested nature of CSR. We thereby do not seek to develop theory or provide an exhaustive review of the literature. Rather, we select those key questions and topics in the contemporary debate on CSR that provide those interested in the concept with a concise and critical introduction to the state-of-the-art of CSR research and practice. In going beyond yet another handbook of 'how to manage' CSR strategy and implementation, we provide readers with a fresh perspective to reflect on how CSR is commonly practised by business firms. By illuminating and scrutinizing present approaches to CSR, this Element aims to provide readers with the ability to understand key concepts in the context of CSR and how businesses attempt to meet the social and environmental expectations of society.

This Element is structured into five sections that each deal with a central question in the CSR debate. First, we ask what the relevant CSR issues are that companies nowadays are confronted with, and what the resulting scope of CSR is. Here, we make a critical distinction between what we call the 'low-hanging fruits of CSR' and the 'high-hanging fruits of CSR'. We further explain the important shift in understanding CSR no longer as 'how the money is spent' but as 'how the money is made'. Second, we ask why companies would pay attention to those issues, illuminating the key drivers and motives for CSR. We unfold two important tensions of the instrumental motive for CSR, namely the 'ethical fallacy' and the 'managerial fallacy', and argue that contemporary CSR is mainly driven by stakeholder expectations that form the institutional infrastructure of CSR. Third, we ask how business firms can implement their CSR commitments into organizational practices and procedures, reviewing important components of the implementation process such as codes of conduct, policies, CSR management frameworks, stakeholder engagement and CSR reporting. We also highlight important complications that are widely observable among business firms in the CSR implementation process. Fourth, we turn to the dark side of CSR and ask why greenwashing and Corporate Social Irresponsibility (CSiR) became common phenomena in the context of CSR. We portray empirical evidence of this and unfold selected theoretical approaches to illustrate some important reasons that help to understand and explain the prevalence of such behaviour. Fifth, in wrapping this Element up, we ask what the key themes are that (should) shape the CSR discussion over the next decade, zooming in on new responsibilities that emerge from digitalization as well as the Sustainable Development Goals (SDGs).

1 What is Corporate Social Responsibility (CSR)? Scope, Issues and Definitional Clarity

The objectives of this section are:

- To introduce key social, environmental and ethical issues to which business firms are confronted and which define the scope of what is commonly understood as Corporate Social Responsibility (CSR).
- To show that CSR is fundamentally about 'how the money is made', in other words about responsibility for harm that emerges along globally expanded value chains. Importantly, CSR is no longer constrained to 'how the money is spent', i.e. limiting CSR to philanthropy or other forms of charitable actions.
- To explain that for understanding CSR in a globalized economy, attention needs to shift from a liability logic based on legal obligations towards the logic of social connection between companies and societal impacts along their supply chain.

1.1 From 'How the Money Is Spent' to 'How the Money Is Made'

Nowadays, hardly a day passes on which we don't hear in the media about yet another corporate scandal, irresponsible behaviour or cases of social, environmental or ethical wrongdoing in which business firms are involved in one way or another. Some of these cases come high on the agenda of public attention, such as working conditions in global textile supply chains in the aftermath of the collapse of the Rana Plaza factory building in April 2013. That day, 1,135 workers of a garment factory in Bangladesh died, and 2,438 were injured because of extremely poor safety conditions and an overcrowded factory building. Such kind of – oftentimes deadly – harm to workers in global supply chains of fashion brands is unfortunately not rare. Rather, the Rana Plaza incident was only a particularly severe case leading to the long necessary public outcry that called for change in the global fashion industry.[1]

However, attributing responsibility for such tragedies is not as easy or straightforward as it might seem. One might indeed ask who is responsible for violations of basic health and safety conditions at the workplace: factory operators flouting national laws? Local governments failing to enforce these laws? Multinational retailers squeezing the last penny out of suppliers? Western consumers unwilling to pay more than a few bucks for a T-shirt? The international community failing to intervene? It may not come as a surprise that much of the subsequent controversy was not primarily directed at the local factory owners, but mainly against powerful Western multinational textile brands such as Adidas, H&M, Inditex (the company behind labels such as Zara and Mango), Primark and the like. Western fashion brands reacted not by denying any sort of responsibility, but rather by acknowledging their linkages to factories violating health and safety conditions.

As a consequence, soon after Rana Plaza, major players in the fashion industry, mainly from Europe, set up an initiative called the Accord on Fire and Building Safety in Bangladesh in May 2013, often referred to as 'the Accord'. This initiative is an independent, legally binding agreement between fashion brands and trade unions designed to work towards a safer garment industry in Bangladesh. Signatories of the Accord pledged to enable a working environment in which basic standards of workplace health and safety measures are implemented and monitored by an independent inspection programme involving retailers, workers, trade unions, local governments as well as non-governmental organizations (NGOs). Furthermore, signatories promised to ensure that safety conditions in involved factories were made publicly available to allow inspections and devise corrective measures in case of breaches of the key health and safety guidelines. In addition, democratically elected health and safety committees were installed in all factories to identify and act on health and safety risks, while worker empowerment was encouraged through training, complaints mechanisms and by giving workers the right to refuse unsafe work. Only a few years later, more than 200 apparel brands had signed the Accord which now covers more than 1,000 Bangladeshi garment factories. Today, six years after the incident, workers' rights are still much of an issue in Bangladesh and other emerging markets.[2] However, the example at least demonstrates that even though global fashion brands are connected to those factories only through complex and globally expanded webs of supply chains and production

---

[1] www.stern.nyu.edu/sites/default/files/assets/documents/con_047408.pdf

[2] https://bhr.stern.nyu.edu/five-years-after-rana-plaza/

networks, they have accepted a responsibility for the health and safety of workers in distant places.

Another example that, relative to the Rana Plaza tragedy, remained somewhat under the radar of large-scale public attention is a 'food drive' organized by US retailer Walmart. The case strikingly illustrates how public perception of social and environmental responsibilities that can be attributed to corporations has changed over the last few decades. According to media reports,[3] for several years some US branches of Walmart organized Thanksgiving food drives for their own employees in order to help those in need by asking co-workers to donate food. At first sight, this may sound like a nice idea. Walmart employees show how much they care about each other by helping their fellow colleagues with too little income to buy their own food to have a nice Thanksgiving dinner. However, as a CNN journalist reported, many workers at Walmart rather felt betrayed by such hypocrisy and the subsequent public outrage came as no surprise.

While local store managers at Walmart may have even acted out of good intention, critics pointed out that according to a report by the National Employment Law Project in 2012,[4] Walmart turned out to be one of the worst-paying companies in the USA. In fact, associates at the company were paid so poorly that they could hardly cover their daily bills, let alone a proper Thanksgiving feast. Critics hence argued that the whole idea and need for organizing such a food drive would not be necessary if Walmart would simply pay their employees a decent wage so that they could afford enough food on their own in the first place. In some way, Walmart was delegating the responsibility for its own employees to its other employees. According to *Forbes* magazine,[5] at the same time Walmart's net income was at around US$17bn, and ample amounts of bonus cheques and stock options have been paid to top management and shareholders.

What do the Rana Plaza factory collapse, the Accord in Bangladesh as well as the Walmart food drive demonstrate about contemporary CSR and the roles and responsibilities of business firms in society? They show how CSR has moved from the idea of 'giving back to society' towards a concept that is about how value is created by a firm, and what the social, environmental and ethical implications of the corresponding value-creating processes are. CSR is no

---

[3] www.forbes.com/sites/rickungar/2013/11/18/walmart-store-holding-thanksgiving-charity-food-drive-for-its-own-employees/#40b69ad02ee5; www.cnbc.com/2014/11/20/wal-mart-defends-employee-food-drive.html

[4] www.nelp.org/content/uploads/2015/03/NELP-Big-Business-Corporate-Profits-Minimum-Wage.pdf

[5] www.forbes.com/sites/clareoconnor/2014/04/15/report-walmart-workers-cost-taxpayers-6-2-billion-in-public-assistance/#39b9d640720b

longer constrained to philanthropy or charity and how the money is spent. According to this logic, companies would maximize their profits without costly adjustments in core business operations, and then compensate for some of the collateral damage by making a few donations to affected stakeholders, as the case of Walmart demonstrates. Today, CSR is elevated to a strategic level and has become fundamentally about how the money is made. Hence, it is about integrating CSR principles in businesses' strategy and core operations that include all parts of the often globally expanded value chain. This includes paying fair wages to workers in distant factories and making sure production processes are socially and environmentally responsible (Wickert et al., 2016). The scope of responsibility is then no longer restricted to the company's headquarters, but is instead stretched along its entire, and often global, supply chain and production network. The Rana Plaza case and the subsequent launch of the Accord demonstrate how CSR has gained strategic relevance in a globalized world.

The expanded scope of CSR brings along a number of complications. As we will show in this Element, disaggregated global supply chains have increasingly replaced the vertically integrated organizational structure that dominated corporations of the twentieth century across multiple industries. While this may allow cost reductions and efficiency gains, it limits a business firm's ability to control and monitor its own supply chains, including labour practices and the very locations from which materials are sourced (Kim & Davis, 2016). Moreover, stakeholders increasingly attribute corporate responsibility *upstream* to actors along the supply chain. This includes those workers in sweatshop factories in Bangladesh that sew shirts for global retailers such as H&M, Nike or Adidas. Moreover, upstream responsibility can go even further to fourth- or fifth-tier suppliers that for instance harvest and deliver raw cotton in the fields of Uzbekistan.[6] Responsibility also reaches *downstream* to consumers and includes the product life cycle. For example, there are potential implications for the environment once products are disposed of as, for instance, in the case of smartphones. Product ingredients may also have implications for consumers, such as food products with high amounts of sodium or trans fats typical in the fast food industry. Figure 1 summarizes these developments.

1.2 From a Liability to a Social Connection-based Understanding of CSR

When considering how CSR has evolved, it appears that stakeholders, including civil society groups, NGOs and consumers, have started to attribute

---

[6] Uzbekistan is a major producer of raw cotton worldwide and has been repeatedly accused of human rights abuses and severe forms of child labour.

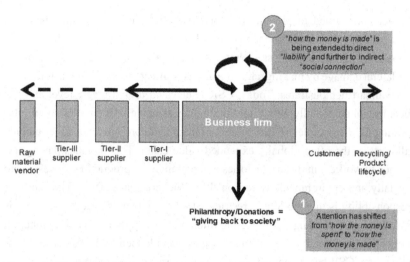

Figure 1: How CSR has transformed from philanthropy to liability to a social connection responsibility.

Source: Own illustration.

responsibility to firms no longer based on liability (i.e. the legal relationship between two entities). Instead, responsibility is increasingly attributed based on a firm's *social connection* to an issue. The liability approach to CSR is based on a legal mindset. Here, responsibility emerges when a legal relationship, and hence an immediately visible causal link between action and harm, can be objectively shown. As the examples above show, holding companies legally responsible is limited when CSR is about how the money is made. This is particularly evident in globally dispersed and highly complex production networks. A clear identification of supply chains is extremely difficult since they involve dozens of steps and unclear or interrupted legal relationships between raw-material producers, vendors, manufacturers, distributors, retailers, and so on. Indeed, over the past decades new communication technologies, low-cost shipping and the liberalization of trade have led many businesses to reconsider their 'make or buy' decisions covering nearly all sectors, from manufacturing to services. As Kim and Davis (2016: p. 1897) have pointed out, 'Nike shoes, Apple phones, and Hewlett-Packard laptops are all manufactured by far-flung contractors, not by the company whose logo is engraved on the product.'

An alternative understanding that offers justification for why and when responsibility emerges is therefore necessary. Evidence suggests that companies have started to acknowledge and act according to this new logic of CSR. While in the past companies used to deny responsibility by pointing to the lack of a legal relationship between themselves and a certain supplier where some harm occurred, the public no longer accepts this. Instead, companies have started to act on a concept of responsibility that instead refers to the consequences of their structural connectedness, the social connection that holds actors 'responsible precisely for things they themselves have *not* done' (Young, 2004: p. 375).

Based on social justice theory, the philosopher Iris Marion Young has developed the concept of social connection (Young, 2004). Her reasoning provides the moral philosophical, rather than legal, basis for thinking about and justifying why and to what extent business firms should meet their social responsibilities in the global marketplace. Her main concern is where firms might create and maintain systemic forms of injustice or harm to distant parties, such as factory workers in Bangladesh or elsewhere. As such, the social connection approach provides an analytical basis for identifying the areas where it is difficult to establish an immediate causal connection between a social, environmental or ethical problem (e.g. low labour standards for supplier factory workers in developing countries) and companies based in other parts of the world. An important assumption here is that systematic disregard of environmental standards or the continuous exploitation of workers and violations of their rights are sources of chronic, rather than incidental, injustices that are linked to the systems and structures of globalized production networks (Schrempf, 2014; Wickert, 2016).

What Young (2004: p. 365) then argues is that companies and also consumers have to 'acknowledge a responsibility with respect to the working conditions of distant workers in other countries, and to take actions to meet such responsibilities'. If companies are said to hold responsibility for the welfare of subcontracted workers in distant places, then this type of responsibility cannot be understood as a legally grounded liability but must be seen as a morally grounded 'political duty'. The liability logic would imply that actors who are directly involved in causing injustice plausibly can be held responsible for the consequences. This may include factory owners, but also governmental authorities that are unwilling or unable to enforce basic laws that protect human rights and labour standards. The case of the Rana Plaza tragedy illustrates that indeed some factory owners had been brought to court and received substantial fines because of their legal responsibility. The problematic aspect in the liability logic, however, is that it allows those companies which have sourced from that factory, including well-known fashion brands such as H&M, to defend themselves by arguing that they did not actually own the factory. In consequence, there has not been an immediate legal relationship to the factory owner, as there are typically multiple subcontractors involved (Young, 2004).

However, stakeholders such as consumers or NGOs no longer accept that powerful global brands can hide behind the excuse of not being legally connected. For example, the Accord in Bangladesh strikingly demonstrates that companies have acknowledged their extended responsibility for global injustice and have taken decisive action. At least among the well-known companies with a valuable brand name to protect, you would hardly find open denial of any sort of responsibility for what happens deep in their supply chain. Young indeed argued that any company's actions partly depend on the actions of others. In other words, 'the scope of an agent's moral obligation extends to all those whom the agent assumes in conducting his or her activity' (Young, 2004, p. 371). This means that any company that sources raw materials or pre-products made under inhumane or environmentally damaging conditions by doing so benefits for instance from low prices that are enabled because of those very conditions. Thus, the beneficiary becomes indirectly connected to some form of injustice. If a company relies on low-priced finished products to gain an edge over its competitors, it implicitly depends on the exploitation of workers who are paid below minimum wages. Young argues that no company can deny this connection to processes of structural injustice and that there is at least a moral, if not a legal, obligation of responsibility.

From an ethical point of view, those who participate in the creation or perpetuation of these structures need to recognize that their actions contribute to this injustice and have to take responsibility for altering these structures in order to prevent or reduce injustices. Civil society and all kinds of stakeholder groups have picked up this basic understanding of why and how responsibilities in global supply chains can and should be attributed and shared – some more explicitly than others. What can be observed is that actions of corporations to be considered legitimate and hence socially acceptable are increasingly related to the idea of social connection. What emerged as a largely ethically grounded rationale has turned into a widespread social expectation that is shared by large parts of public audiences.

1.3 The Low- and High-hanging Fruits of CSR

If we take the social connection approach as a basis for justifying that certain responsibilities exist, then what will be the relevant CSR issues that have emerged on the corporate radar? They would certainly stretch the scope of CSR beyond issues such as philanthropy or building a kindergarten at the corporate headquarters. Indeed, the contemporary understanding of CSR suggests that attention has shifted from what could be called the 'low-hanging fruits' to what can better be described as 'high-hanging fruits' (see e.g. Wickert et al., 2016; Wickert & de Bakker, 2018).

Low-hanging fruits are certainly not unimportant and often also have significant social or environmental impacts. They include things such as pollution control, eco-efficiency and waste management, granting employee benefits such as free lunch or health benefits. Hence, they typically describe issues that reach comparably low up or down the supply chain. We can define low-hanging fruits as those issues where a connection to core business operations is directly visible because they are in a company's immediate sphere of influence. Often, they are even simply mandated by law, such as environmental or health and safety regulations. Because of this, low-hanging fruits generally allow for easily establishing a business case (i.e. enhanced profits through higher sales or reduced costs) in terms of straightforward and inexpensive behavioural and material changes. Tackling such issues then leads to a directly measurable effect with clear financial benefits for the company. Research suggests that many companies indeed begin their CSR journey by addressing low-hanging fruits (e.g. Baumann-Pauly et al., 2013).

Sharma and Henriques (2005: p. 158) studied the Canadian forestry industry and their findings reflect what can be found in many other industries as well: companies are well positioned in the 'early stages of sustainability performance such as pollution control and eco-efficiency'. However, more fundamental changes in business models that would involve the redefinition of business ecosystems and which would require substantial investments in organizational systems and processes are still 'in their infancy'.

Turning to the high-hanging fruits, as the example of the forestry industry suggests, becomes progressively more difficult and often requires large-scale changes and reconsideration of production processes, or for instance entirely new technologies and buyer-supplier relationships. For example, a telecommunications company such as Vodafone may place recycling bins in its shops to collect used smartphones. This may seem like a nice gesture, but it certainly remains a low-hanging fruit. Cost implications for Vodafone are relatively low, the measure is far away from a reconsideration of its business model, and responsibility is basically delegated away to consumers to actually return their used phones. However, the real CSR challenge would be to reduce the number of smartphones sold and then thrown away after only a year or so in the first place. This, however, is fundamentally against the business model of many telecommunications providers and how they are currently marketing their products. On top of that, making sure phones are not produced under inhumane conditions using so-called conflict minerals is an even more complex problem.

So what are these high-hanging fruits? Conflict minerals are a case in point that has been gaining more attention by the public as well as by companies and governments (Reinecke & Ansari, 2016). When thinking of Vodafone or one of its competitors, social and ecological problems connected to the mining of minerals very well underscore that a liability logic needs to be replaced by a social connection approach. To illustrate the idea of high-hanging fruits based on the social connection logic, let us take the example of smartphones and other electronic devices that nowadays nearly everyone uses. Where does the production of a smartphone actually begin? It begins with the extraction of raw minerals in mines, many of them located in some of the world's poorest regions such as Central Africa.

Conflict minerals are natural resources extracted in zones of armed conflict and sold to finance and perpetuate the conflict. One of the most prominent examples has been the eastern provinces of the Democratic Republic of the Congo, where various armies and rebel groups have profited from mining operations while contributing to violence and exploitation during wars in the region (Global Witness, 2017). Beyond Congo, mineral trading has funded some of the world's most brutal conflicts for decades and fuelled human rights abuses in areas such as Afghanistan, Colombia, Mexico and Zimbabwe. The four most commonly mined conflict minerals (known as 3TGs, from their initials) are cassiterite (for tin), wolframite (for tungsten), coltan (for tantalum), and gold ore. So-called blood diamonds are also often mentioned alongside the problems associated with conflict minerals, as they are typically mined under similarly horrifying conditions. These minerals and jewels enter global supply chains and are essential in the manufacture of a variety of devices, including consumer electronics such as mobile phones, laptops, and MP3 players as well as jewellery and batteries for electric cars. Because of the highly complex webs of supply chain relations and multiple intermediaries, it is very difficult for consumers to know whether their favourite products fund armed conflicts (Kim & Davis, 2016).

Next to being a source of funding for armed conflicts, the conditions under which the minerals are being mined are extremely problematic. Unsafe working conditions and work-related injuries and deaths, forced and child labour, corruption as well as other systemic human rights abuses are the norm (Global Witness, 2017; Kim & Davis, 2016; Reinecke & Ansari, 2016). Conflict minerals mining therefore represents a striking case of 'modern slavery' (Crane, 2013). While we may think that such things as slavery might be something from the dark side of history long overcome, forms of modern slavery continue to exist. Such forms of slavery occur if the following conditions are met: people are (1) forced to work through threat; (2) owned or are controlled by an 'employer', particularly through mental, physical or threatened abuse; (3) de-humanized and treated as a resource; (4) physically constrained or restricted in freedom of movement; (5) subject to economic exploitation through underpayment (Crane, 2013: p. 51). According to a report[7] of the International Labour Organization (ILO) from 2017, modern forms of slavery affect more than 40 million people, including almost 25 million in forced labour, and more than 15 million in forced marriage. Twenty-five per cent of the victims are typically children. Out of those trapped in forced labour, 16 million are exploited in the private sector including domestic work, construction, agriculture or mining. Other forms include forced sexual exploitation and forced labour imposed by state authorities.

Modern slavery in the context of conflict minerals has led to increased public awareness and strong campaigning by NGOs such as Global Witness, urging governments around the world to act and address the problem of conflict minerals. In June 2016, after years of negotiations, the European Union (EU) reached a political understanding on a new regulation which is intended to break the links between the minerals trade, armed conflicts and widespread and systematic human rights abuses. The EU regulation focuses on conflict-affected or high-risk areas, which refer to regions in a state of armed conflict, fragile post-conflict areas, or areas with weak or non-existent governance and security, such as failed states. Similar regulations emerged in the USA under the Dodd Frank Act of 2010.

To meet these new regulations, firms will be required to demonstrate that they have sourced their minerals responsibly and transparently. Stakeholders including the Organisation for Economic Co-operation and Development (OECD), the European Commission as well as NGOs such as Global Witness have elaborated a process of due diligence to support companies in checking their supply chains and ensuring that they prevent conflict minerals from entering global markets. Due diligence thus describes an ongoing process through which companies can identify whether the minerals they purchase or handle have been linked to human rights abuses, conflict or corruption, and put in place strategies and management systems to mitigate these risks. Due diligence also includes carrying out independent third-party audits and annually reporting on progress. As a concept, it is based upon the premise that companies have a responsibility to ensure that they do not benefit on the back of serious harm to individuals, societies or the environment. At the same time, both the EU and the OECD, which have played a key role in developing the due diligence framework, emphasize that all companies buying, selling or handling any minerals should conduct due diligence on their supply chains. Notably, however, the extent and nature of an appropriate level of due diligence for each company depends on individual circumstances, such as the size of the company, its sector, location

---

[7] www.ilo.org/global/publications/books/WCMS_575479/lang–en/index.htm

and position in the supply chain. In other words, Apple's due diligence should look very different from that of a one-person operation run out of Kigali, Rwanda. Similarly, the due diligence process of the global diamond miner and trader De Beers should differ significantly from that of a jewellery designer based in Antwerp, Belgium.

Overall, the case of conflict minerals demonstrates some of the high-hanging fruits and upstream responsibilities with regard to the complex production processes of many of the electronic devices we use on a daily basis. It becomes even more complicated when looking downstream: when we buy a new phone once a year, the old one will end up somewhere. Indeed, according to investigations[8] of the ILO, e-waste is currently the largest-growing waste stream, exceeding 50 million tons annually. It is hazardous, complex and expensive to treat e-waste in an environmentally sound manner, and there is a general lack of legislation or enforcement surrounding it. Most e-waste ends up in the general waste stream without proper recycling. Eighty per cent of the e-waste in developed countries sent for recycling ends up being shipped (often illegally) to developing countries to be recycled by hundreds of thousands of informal workers. Such globalization of e-waste has adverse environmental and health implications. Open landfills abound in countries such as Ghana where workers are exposed to hazardous substances released on vast unofficial waste dumps, lacking basic protective clothing and health and safety measures. Compared to the case of conflict-minerals, the topic of e-waste is still marginal in terms of public attention and actions taken by companies. It remains to be seen what actions will be taken by civil society, governments and firms to address yet another high-hanging fruit of CSR.

1.4 CSR in the Context of Globalization

It is no surprise that these issues and ideas about the new roles and responsibilities of business in society have reached the corporate world. Even more so, businesses are nowadays under ever-increasing pressure and public scrutiny. In light of the severity of issues such as conflict minerals, and reoccurring scandals, misbehaviour, fraud and greenwashing, even management gurus such as Michael Porter have concluded that 'the capitalist system is under siege. In recent years business increasingly has been viewed as a major cause of social, environmental, and economic problems. Companies are widely perceived to be prospering at the expense of the broader community' (Porter & Kramer, 2011: p. 64). In consequence, Porter continues, 'The legitimacy of business [i.e. the

---

[8] www.ilo.org/sector/Resources/publications/WCMS_196105/lang–en/index.htm

societal acceptance of what businesses do and how responsibly they behave] has fallen to levels not seen in recent history' (p. 64).

As the prominence of CSR and its entering into the corporate boardroom underscores, the business world has reacted. In order to gain back the legitimacy and trust of the broader public, business firms began to develop comprehensive CSR profiles. While the idea of social responsibility was not entirely new, however, in particular since the end of the twentieth century, the way CSR is understood and practised is influenced by three key developments. *First*, in the course of globalization, the political influence of national states has been waning. In what has been called the 'postnational constellation' (Habermas, 2001), national governments have limited control over corporations operating on a global scale and are thus not always able to safeguard the social well-being of their citizens. *Second*, civil society has developed a much stronger social and environmental awareness, often a result of the political campaigns of activists. Compared to traditional party politics, such campaigns provide an alternative means of addressing topics such as social inequality, ecological destruction, or climate change.

Third, the increasing influence of financial markets on economic success (often referred to as the 'financialization' of the economy) and the growing mobility of corporations have induced an economic shift (Scherer & Palazzo, 2007). For example, in order to circumvent high taxation or exploit low wages, firms relocate their headquarters to countries considered as tax havens or where they can afford to pay the lowest possible wages or benefit from lax environmental standards. The failure to address global warming is a case in point where multinational corporations (MNCs) have the chance to arbitrate among alternative regulations. They can escape strict regulations by moving their operations or supply activities to countries with rather low standards (e.g. to lower their tax burden or cost of production). All of this has led to a 'globalization of responsibility' and calls for alternative ways to regulate global business activity. Reinforced by media pressure and information technology, these three developments have led to the claim that business should assume more economic, social, environmental and ethical responsibility.

Figure 2 illustrates how the CSR landscape has changed due to the process of globalization. First, the relationship between the three most important societal actors – business firms and the private sector more generally, nation states and governmental authorities, and civil society – has been fundamentally transformed. Second, new players have been formed or (re)entered the playing field, such as self-regulatory initiatives of the private sector, transnational organizations and associated initiatives such as the United Nations Global Compact (UNGC), or multi-stakeholder initiatives (MSIs) such as the Forest Stewardship Council (FSC). We will explain these developments in greater detail below.

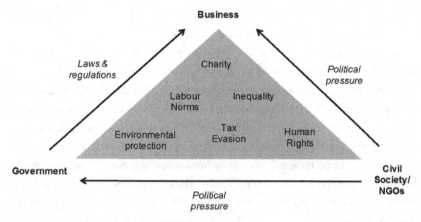

Figure 2: Relationships between business, governments and civil society in the context of globalization.

Source: Own illustration.

1.5 Towards a Political Understanding of CSR

In order to understand the assumptions and foundations of the transformation of CSR in a globalized economy, it is useful to distinguish it from traditional conceptualizations. Before the turn of the century, scholars of CSR generally held the assumption of relatively homogeneous societal expectations, functioning nation states, and democratic institutions that can provide and enforce regulatory frameworks to guide business conduct (for an overview, see Windsor, 2006). This perspective reflects the classical 'Friedmanian' view on CSR. Back in 1970, economics Nobel laureate Milton Friedman published a now (in)famous essay in which he proclaimed that the only responsibility of business firms is to increase their profits for the benefit of shareholders, and that it should be the responsibility of governments to ensure societal welfare (Friedman, 1970). According to Friedman, corporations should not undertake social policies and programmes because this is what governments are supposed to do. Governments are elected by the public to pursue social goals whereas corporate managers are acting on behalf of shareholders, so their accountability is primarily to shareholders, not to the public.

Based on this assumption Friedman proposes a strict political division of labour in society – corporations pursue economic goals, while governments pursue social goals. It could be argued that his argument was defensible because when the original article was published, globalization and the transnational integration of the economy were at significantly lower levels than today. At the same time, Friedman's understanding of CSR corresponds largely with what we now consider as philanthropy or charity, or what we have described as 'how the money is spent'. More recently, the question of the wider responsibilities of business has, however, become far more complex, and societal stakeholders are concerned about how the money is made. Moreover, today, we observe that corporations have taken on or are expected to take a role in society that overlaps and interferes quite substantially with that of governments. This happens mainly in three areas that reflect so-called regulatory gaps (see also Crane & Matten, 2015):

1. *Governments are no longer providing basic social needs*: In the past, tasks such as the provision of water, electricity, education, healthcare, basic transportation, public safety and telecommunication were largely considered a fundamental role of governments in exchange for tax earnings. Yet, in consequence of what might be called a neo-liberal watershed of privatization, liberalization and deregulation, services such as water provision have been privatized in many countries and are hence in the hands of companies. When companies take responsibility for important issues such as people's health and sanitation, a somewhat more complex social responsibility arises. In fact, companies in these new areas face many of the societal expectations hitherto directed at governments and the political sphere in general.

2. *Governments are unable or unwilling to address social needs*: Particularly in less-developed countries, businesses often deal with government authorities that lack the resources to cater effectively for basic social needs, even though they are formally entitled to do so. To compensate for this, companies have started to build roads, housing, schools, and hospitals for the communities in which they operate, or they compensate for the lack of effective regulation by launching business-led soft-law initiatives. In consequence, corporations often replace governments and hence face social expectations that typically would be placed on the government.

3. *Governments cannot address social problems beyond national boundaries*: Financial markets, climate change, or the Internet are new social spaces that no single government can control alone. Rather, these spaces are often influenced and governed by businesses. Consequently, the public expects businesses to address climate change, internet privacy or uncontrollable financial markets as a natural consequence of the global reach of these problems.

All three developments have led to a situation where businesses find themselves facing societal expectations that are similar to those usually reserved for political authorities. An increasing number of business firms are confronted with such regulatory gaps, that is, contexts where social and environmental standards are low or not enforced by governmental authorities (Matten & Crane,

2005; Scherer & Palazzo, 2007). Based on the observation that corporations in such contexts do not just avoid, but jointly with actors from civil society, governments and international organizations, increasingly 'fill' regulatory gaps, a conceptualization of CSR has been developed that promotes a view of corporations as *political actors*. In this context, one of the most notable conceptions addressing the evolving globalization of CSR has been promoted under the label of 'political CSR' (e.g. Scherer & Palazzo, 2007). Political CSR, in a nutshell, assumes a broad, potentially global sphere of influence of corporations and assigns them responsibility for those environmental and social externalities to which they are socially connected – that is, for problems 'to which [corporations] contribute by their actions and ... from which they themselves benefit, and which they have encouraged or tolerated through their own behaviour' (Scherer & Palazzo, 2011, p. 913).

Corporations are urged, for instance by NGOs, to proactively engage in self-regulatory activities which provide specific norms and guidance in relation to global social and environmental problems. For example, globally operating firms are expected to ensure labour rights of workers in distant factories, or to uphold environmentally friendly means of production at the locations where they source raw materials. By engaging in matters hitherto regulated by the state, corporations become increasingly politicized, which means that a strict division of labour between private business and nation states is blurring (Matten & Crane, 2005). To overcome the democratic deficit inherent in such political engagement of private actors, corporations need to enter into a dialogue with a variety of stakeholders. In short, in political CSR 'corporate attention and money' are redirected to 'societal challenges beyond immediate stakeholder pressure'. Moreover, decision-making processes need to reflect the interests of civil society and those affected by their actions, all of which calls for a democratization of business conduct (Scherer & Palazzo, 2007: p. 1115).

1.6 Multiple Actors Enter the CSR Arena

What do these more theoretical arguments and the notion of political CSR imply for those actors that have entered the field? As we will see, next to businesses themselves, multiple players influence and give direction to what CSR entails and what businesses need to do to address CSR strategically. All of these actors have a certain agenda and interests they represent and pursue, and shape how CSR is understood and practised by corporations. They can be categorized into five groups of actors: international organizations, civil society organizations, business-driven self-regulatory initiatives, cross-sector MSIs, and governments.

First, we can observe that international organizations play an important role. This includes the United Nations (UN), the OECD, the ILO and the World Bank, all of which have embarked on the CSR agenda and have proposed ideas and policies that generally aim to establish global rules for private actors, so-called soft law. One of the most famous CSR initiatives that deserves special attention and which emerged under the umbrella of an international organization, the UN, is the United Nations Global Compact (UNGC).

Back in 1999 at the World Economic Forum, then Secretary-General of the UN Kofi Annan announced a 'Global Compact' to invite business firms around the globe to work together for sustainable development. Less than a year later, the UN Global Compact Office was founded to promote responsible business practices among the global business community.[9] By 2019, it became the world's largest CSR initiative with about 13,000 members in more than 170 countries bringing together stakeholders from the private sector, civil society, academia, and governments. According to its website the UNGC is a 'call to companies to align strategies and operations with universal principles on human rights, labour, environment and anti-corruption, and take actions that advance societal goals' such as the UN Sustainable Development Goals (SDGs), as well as report on their implementation. The goals of the UNGC rest fundamentally on the idea of CSR being about how the money is made. The UNGC suggests that CSR starts with a company's value system and by incorporating the ten principles of the UNGC into strategies, policies and procedures, and establishing a culture of integrity. This means operating in ways that, at a minimum, meet fundamental responsibilities in the areas of human rights, labour, environment and anti-corruption. Responsible businesses enact the same values and principles wherever they have a presence and know that good practices in one area do not offset harm in another. The ten principles are universal, as they are derived from the Universal Declaration of Human Rights, the ILO's Declaration on Fundamental Principles and Rights at Work, the Rio Declaration on Environment and Development, and the United Nations Convention Against Corruption (see Table 1).

These principles are important for understanding the scope of CSR as for many business firms they serve as the 'moral compass' that guides companies and other stakeholders in setting the agenda. The principles are helpful because they point out the main areas in which regulatory gaps can occur and to which a company may be socially connected through its supply chain. We will get back to the UNGC throughout this Element, for instance when discussing the implementation of CSR principles in core business processes and procedures in

---

[9] www.unglobalcompact.org

Table 1: The ten principles of the UNGC.

Human rights	
Principle 1	Businesses should support and respect the protection of internationally proclaimed human rights; and
Principle 2	make sure that they are not complicit in human rights abuses.
Labour	
Principle 3	Businesses should uphold the freedom of association and the effective recognition of the right to collective bargaining;
Principle 4	the elimination of all forms of forced and compulsory labour;
Principle 5	the effective abolition of child labour; and
Principle 6	the elimination of discrimination in respect of employment and occupation.
Environment	
Principle 7	Businesses should support a precautionary approach to environmental challenges;
Principle 8	undertake initiatives to promote greater environmental responsibility; and
Principle 9	encourage the development and diffusion of environmentally friendly technologies.
Anti-corruption	
Principle 10	Businesses should work against corruption in all its forms, including extortion and bribery.

Source: www.unglobalcompact.org.

Section 3, but also in Section 4 when we critically examine some pitfalls and challenges linked to the way the UNGC is structured.

Second, civil society organizations have been putting significantly more pressure on corporations to act socially and environmentally responsible. NGOs operating at a local or global level aim to police corporations where governments fail to do so. A famous example of a globally known NGO is Greenpeace. The main objective of this NGO is to safeguard the natural environment and raise awareness of issues such as climate change and how the private sector might either accelerate or mitigate this problem. Another well-known NGO is Amnesty International, working for the promotion of human rights around the globe. Often, the strategies of NGOs include 'naming and shaming' irresponsible behaviour of businesses. NGOs target firms through campaigns or call for product boycotts when certain very unsustainable actions have been detected, such as Greenpeace's campaign against Nestlé's alleged destruction of the rainforest in Borneo. Other NGOs, such as the World Wide Fund for Nature (WWF) are less confrontational and seek strategic partnerships with specific MNCs in order to address a problematic issue. WWF and The Coca-Cola Company are for instance engaged in a partnership to help conserve the world's freshwater resources.

Third, we can observe a steady increase in the number of self-regulatory initiatives formed by corporations and explicitly addressing various CSR challenges. Through these initiatives, the private sector and corporate members take on quasi-governmental roles and develop rules and procedures to regulate, for instance, working conditions in the textile industry (see the earlier example of the Accord in Bangladesh). Famous examples include the World Business Council for Sustainable Development (WBCSD) and the Business Social Compliance Initiative (BSCI). The WBCSD for instance is a CEO-led global advocacy institution of around 200 MNCs to advance knowledge and share best practices of business involvement in sustainable development.

Fourth, many cross-sector MSIs have emerged that have overlapping objectives with self-regulatory initiatives by businesses, but with an important difference: they include not only private sector members, but are open also to members from different civil society groups. MSIs are thus more democratic than self-regulatory initiatives and are guided by the principle of equal participation. The FSC is one of the most prominent examples that tackles a global regulatory gap, namely the protection of forests by avoiding deforestation and promoting sustainable forestry. The FSC demonstrates how business decisions became embedded in a context of democratic governance and problem-solving by bringing not only corporations but also NGOs and multiple civil society groups to the table. This includes well-known corporations such as IKEA, Home Depot, and OBI, environmental NGOs such as WWF or Greenpeace, but also many smaller local human rights activist and indigenous peoples groups.

Together, FSC members developed a set of principles and criteria for the sustainable management of forests that applies on a global basis, including monitoring and certification. Many timber products worldwide feature the FSC certification logo and signal to consumers that the materials used in the product stem from a sustainably managed forest. Scherer and Palazzo (2007) suggest that the FSC can be considered one of the most advanced concepts reflecting a political understanding of CSR. This is because the FSC illustrates some of the key aspects of a politically embedded corporation. In fact, corporate FSC members address an important environmental challenge that national governments are not able or willing to tackle alone. Self-regulation takes place in a broad process of democratic will formation in collaboration with civil society actors. The independent third-party certification enforces a democratic control of corporate activities.

Fifth, while we have emphasized the emergence and prominent role of non-government players in the CSR landscape and governmental influence shrinking relative to that of the private sector and civil society, governments still play an important role and have been reacting to these developments in different manners (Kourula et al., 2019). This is interesting, as most of the discussion on political CSR was based on the assumption that governments generally retreat and become less important as actors shaping the CSR agenda. However, particularly in recent years, various governmental agencies of nation states have aimed to 'reclaim' some of the lost territory by re-entering the CSR playing field. On the one hand, demands for social responsibilities of businesses have become more demanding when looking at how CSR is defined by the public. In 2001, the European Commission proposed its first definition of CSR. In a Green Paper,[10] it is stated that CSR is 'a concept whereby companies integrate social and environmental concerns in their business operations and in their interaction with their stakeholders on a voluntary basis'. Two components of this definition are important. First, the definition refers to social and environmental concerns, while not being very precise about what those actually are. Second, the definition emphasizes that this should happen on a voluntary basis. As the updated definition of the European Commission released in 2011[11] shows, public expectations about the scope of CSR became much more demanding: 'CSR is the responsibility of enterprises for their impacts on society. To fully meet their social responsibility, enterprises should have in place a process to integrate social, environmental, ethical, human rights and consumer concerns into their business operations and core strategy in close collaboration with their stakeholders'.[12] While the voluntary nature of CSR is no longer emphasized, the range of issues under the umbrella of CSR is significantly expanded and their connection to core business operations is made explicit.

On the other hand, governments are re-entering the game by trying to push forward several new laws and regulations in light of the failure or lacking effectiveness of many market-based initiatives. This reflects a shift back from the 'soft-law' (i.e. voluntary and non-binding) approach that was praised by the private sector back to 'hard law' (i.e. non-voluntary and binding). A central argument of governments to introduce hard law was that many of those

---

[10] European Commission Green Paper (2001). Promoting a European Framework for Corporate Social Responsibility. http://europa.eu/rapid/press-release_DOC-01-9_en.pdf

[11] European Commission (2011). A renewed EU strategy 2011–2014 for Corporate Social Responsibility. http://www.europarl.europa.eu/meetdocs/2009_2014/documents/com/com_com(2011)0681_/com_com(2011)0681_en.pdf

[12] Ibid.

voluntary initiatives have been ineffective in actually solving or at least mitigating some of the most severe social and environmental problems. Thus, while most of the attention of both researchers as well as companies was on the 'privatization' of governance and the emergence of private self-regulation (i.e. shifting authority away from governments to private actors and civil society), recently the trend seems to have been reversed (see Kourula et al., 2019 for an overview). For instance, linked to the case of conflict minerals we discussed earlier, the EU, the USA and other nations have passed laws about the handling of and reporting on conflict minerals, putting an expanded set of demands on businesses. Likewise, legislation about social and environmental reporting is on its way in the EU[13] and other countries, obliging companies to publish yearly reports about the progress they have made with regard to their CSR objectives. The US Foreign Corrupt Practices Act even allows the US government to sue corporations (even non-US ones) for offering or accepting bribes in another country. These efforts show that governments are (re-)entering the CSR arena and are likely to significantly shape the future agenda much more than they did in the past.

1.7 Defining CSR

After having discussed these developments and players in the CSR arena, we will now develop a definition of CSR. Given the complexity of the social, environmental and ethical challenges that lie ahead, and the multiplicity of actors involved, it seems that finding a one-size-fits-all definition for CSR is impossible. Indeed, scholars have struggled with this ever since the term CSR emerged. In a seminal study, Matten and Moon (2008: p. 405) have argued that there are at least three reasons for this complication: first, CSR is an essentially contested concept that is defined (and applied) differently by different groups of people in different contexts. It might of course be that this ambiguity about appropriate terminology is the reason why the idea of CSR has been successful. If stakeholders cannot agree upon the meaning of CSR and specify its scope precisely, business firms could easily take advantage of this by selectively framing CSR against those issues areas that they can conveniently address. This relates particularly to the low-hanging fruits where a company might for instance argue that CSR is mainly about things such as eco-efficiency. What is nevertheless a uniting feature of the label CSR is that stakeholders – even if they disagree on its precise meaning – have for decades concurred on the importance of debating the role of business in society.

---

[13] https://ec.europa.eu/info/business-economy-euro/company-reporting-and-auditing/company-reporting/non-financial-reporting_en

Second, CSR overlaps with other concepts that describe the business–society relationship, such as business ethics, corporate sustainability, or corporate citizenship. While different and important nuances exist and need to be acknowledged (e.g. business ethics is generally concerned with questions of right or wrong; sustainability is generally concerned with systemwide ecological implications), all of these concepts have at their root the fundamental question of the role of business in society (see Bansal & Song, 2017 for an overview). Finally, as with many other forms of business organization and governance, CSR is a dynamic phenomenon. What counts as an issue relevant to the CSR debate changes over time, as new problems emerge and formerly novel practices become routine. Such change is for instance evident from the shift in the scope of CSR from how the money is spent to how the money is made.

Despite these challenges it is important to have an, albeit broad, working definition for CSR. In this Element, we therefore define CSR as follows:

> *Corporate Social Responsibility (CSR) is an umbrella term to describe how business firms, small and large, integrate social, environmental and ethical responsibilities to which they are connected into their core business strategies, structures and procedures within and across divisions, functions as well as value chains in collaboration with relevant stakeholders.*

This definition emphasizes several important characteristics of CSR. First, the definition does not emphasize that CSR is a voluntary concept. Many prominent definitions point out the voluntary character of CSR with regard to actions *beyond the law*. What we can observe, however, is that in the global business environment CSR became a de facto requirement and new laws such as those we reviewed are emerging. Moreover, CSR has become a necessary component of business conduct to ensure legitimacy and a firm's social licence to operate. Even the European Commission removed the word voluntary from its new definition of CSR to emphasize that CSR is a response to societal expectations. Hence, it is nowadays hard to find firms without any sort of CSR activities, often based on industrywide standards. In particular, what we will discuss in Section 2 is that the development towards a mainstream management concept is accompanied by the circumstance that CSR has been pushed much beyond purely voluntary actions.

Second, CSR is a multi-actor concept and inherently stakeholder-driven. Business firms are seen as embedded in a web of stakeholder relations and confronted with oftentimes diverging interests to which they react in one way or another. CSR thus involves considering a range of interests and impacts among a variety of different stakeholders other than just shareholders. The assumption that firms have responsibilities to shareholders is usually not contested, but the point is that because corporations rely on various other constituencies such as consumers, employees, suppliers, and local communities in order to survive and prosper, they do not *only* have responsibilities, or 'fiduciary duties', to shareholders. While many disagree on how much emphasis should be given to shareholders in the CSR debate, and on the extent to which other stakeholders should be taken into account, it is the expanding of corporate responsibility to these other groups that characterizes much of the essential nature of CSR.

Next, we explicitly did not use the term 'corporation', but 'business firms, large and small' in our definition. This is to highlight that CSR is not an idea restricted to large multinational corporations. While the term has emerged in mainstream discussions about the role of business in society and will hence be used for the sake of congruence, it should not be forgotten that also small- and medium-sized enterprises (SMEs) have responsibilities towards society, and that they might be connected to the same social and environmental challenges as large firms (Wickert, 2016). While SMEs are generally defined as not having more than 250 employees, they make up the vast majority of businesses in nearly every economy worldwide. In fact, often up to 99 per cent of all registered businesses are SMEs. Research has pointed out that the CSR activities of smaller firms are different to those in large firms in a number of ways (Baumann-Pauly et al., 2013; Wickert et al., 2016). Typically, owner-managers and their values and beliefs play a more important role than external influences or instrumental considerations to which large firms are more exposed. CSR in SMEs is more informal and more connected to local communities and immediate stakeholders. At the same time, SMEs as much as MNCs are in many cases challenged by similar problems such as working conditions in their suppliers' factories. For instance, in the textile industry, many SMEs source from exactly the same factories that MNCs do, and while being small might evoke a different way of addressing a social or environmental problem, the social connection is the same. The same basic principles about human rights equally apply to all corporations regardless of their size or the geographic location of their activities.

Lastly, CSR must be understood as a multidimensional construct. That is, even though it includes the word 'social', CSR is generally understood as equally being concerned about environmental and ethical issues. This reflects the internationally agreed view that the responsibilities business firms have towards society encompass four key issue areas: human rights (as determined in the Universal Declaration of Human Rights), labour rights (as stated in the ILO's Declaration on Fundamental Principles and Rights at Work), environmental principles (as agreed upon in the Rio Declaration on Environment and Development), as well as anti-corruption (as stated in the UN Convention

Against Corruption). These four issue areas that are also reflected in the ten principles of the UN Global Compact should not be seen as an exhaustive and definite list of responsibilities. Rather, they form a moral compass, outlining minimum standards when discussing what should be expected from business firms. We will discuss in the final section of this Element how newly emerging issues such as the SDGs, but also the digitalization of the economy, bring about a set of new issues that will most likely shape the agenda and content of CSR over the next decades.

1.8 Summary

In this section we have addressed the fundamental question of what CSR is and which social, environmental and ethical issues it entails. Fundamentally, CSR is about how companies earn their profits and not how they distribute them. Further, we have shown where those issues can appear along global value chains, classifying them into low- and high-hanging fruits. We have argued that globalized production networks are a key factor that stretches the sphere of business responsibility towards those issues, impacts and consequences with which they are socially connected. The changing relationship between governments and private business firms leads to a fundamental shift in how social and environmental responsibilities are understood. To address these CSR challenges in the context of globalization, scholars have proposed a political understanding of CSR that brings along a range of actors into the arena and with which business firms are urged to collaborate in various ways. We have ended the section with a broad definition of CSR. In the next section, we will elaborate the motives that businesses have to engage with CSR and address those issues we have outlined. We will argue that there are ethical, instrumental and stakeholder-driven motives for CSR that bring about various challenges in how CSR is implemented in strategies and procedures.

2 Why Would Business Firms Engage in CSR? Motives and Drivers Beyond the Business Case

The objectives of this section are:

- To address the question of why businesses are motivated to engage in CSR, based on ethical, instrumental, and relational considerations.
- To outline the ethical driver for CSR that is based on moral considerations and the understanding of CSR as 'the right thing to do'.
- To introduce the business case for CSR as an instrumental driver that is based on the principle of 'doing well by doing good'; and to outline two important

fallacies of this approach: the *ethical fallacy* and the *managerial fallacy* of the business case for CSR.

- To illustrate the relational driver for CSR that generally aims to ensure a firm's licence to operate and societal legitimacy. This driver is based on pressures external to the firm stemming from stakeholders and the institutional environment and has become the most important motive that explains why firms engage in CSR.

In Section 1, we unfolded the scope of CSR by discussing the various social, environmental and ethical issues that fall under the umbrella of CSR. We explained how those issues have expanded over the last few decades from philanthropic and charitable actions towards the 'high-hanging fruits' that appear in businesses' core operations as well as their global value chains and production networks, such as human rights violations, modern forms of slavery, or climate change and environmental pollution. In Section 2, we will expand on this by addressing the fundamental question of why firms would engage in CSR in the first place. We will delve into the various and dynamic motives that explain CSR engagement. Following the literature, we will divide our analysis into three broad motives, namely 'ethical', 'instrumental', and 'relational', all of which influence managerial decision-making for CSR to varying degrees.

2.1 Ethical Motives for CSR

The ethical motive for CSR generally suggests that business firms take up responsibility because it is 'the right thing to do' from a moral point of view. This approach marks the historical beginning of the debate about what the social responsibilities of businesses are. Discussions of philanthropic responsibilities of business owners date back to the days of early industrialists such as Rockefeller and Carnegie in the USA, or Alfred Krupp in Germany, who donated large portions of their wealth to charitable causes such as education, healthcare and culture. Recently, the issue has resurged in light of modern-day philanthropists such as Mark Zuckerberg with his Chan Zuckerberg Initiative, or Bill Gates with his Bill & Melinda Gates Foundation. Critics argue that rising influence of individuals on public welfare undermines democracy and puts the provision of many public services at the discretion of those philanthropists who are not legitimated by public vote. While we have argued that philanthropy should rather be considered an outdated approach to CSR because it is not based on the premise of how the money is made, rather than spent, it nevertheless stood at the beginning of an important discussion that led to the development of the contemporary understanding of CSR.

The birth of what we now understand as CSR is generally associated with the works of Howard R. Bowen and his seminal book *The Social Responsibilities of the Businessman* from the early 1950s (1953). Bowen set forth an initial definition of what came to be known as CSR: 'It refers to the (ethical) obligations of businessmen to pursue those policies, to make those decisions, or to follow those lines of action which are desirable in terms of the objectives and values of our society.' Thus, the definition is explicitly linked to the moral obligations of businessmen beyond economic performance. At the same time, it acknowledges that what is morally right and wrong is largely determined by those external societal expectations which still matter a great deal today. Business responsibility then is the 'social consciousness' of managers who are responsible for the consequences of their actions in a sphere wider than what is covered by their profit-and-loss statements. Importantly, at the time the focus was largely on individual responsibility of presumably male decision-makers in organizations and their ability for informed ethical judgement, rather than on looking at a company as a whole. This idea of personal responsibility was influential in the early days of CSR and has been picked up in the literature since then, for instance by outlining the distinct personal values of managers as drivers for CSR (e.g. Hemingway & Maclagan, 2004).

However, discussions about the ethical motive for CSR soon moved to the organizational level of analysis. Influential in this regard is the work of Archie B. Carroll (1991) and his 'pyramid of CSR' that conceptualizes the management of organizational stakeholders based on moral justification. Carroll depicted a four-stage pyramid structure of CSR, in which economic responsibilities ('be profitable') lay at the foundation of all business behaviour. On top of that, and somewhat narrower as we move up the pyramid, were legal responsibilities ('obey the law'). Carroll argued that the law reflects society's codification of right and wrong, and businesses were obliged to play by the rules of the game – based on the important assumption that governments are actually able to enforce those rules of the game. Further up were ethical responsibilities ('be ethical') that comprised businesses' obligation to do what is right, just and fair, and to avoid harm to stakeholders. On top of the pyramid, markedly the narrowest spot, came philanthropic responsibilities ('be a good corporate citizen') where businesses should contribute resources to their communities to improve the overall quality of life and welfare.

The pyramid of CSR also has been very influential in shaping the CSR debate, but holds a number of important limitations. First, with its focus on ethical responsibilities it pays only limited attention to the socio-cultural heterogeneity of what is right and wrong in the global context, as well as how to address more systemic problems and structural injustices linked to the nature of capitalism. Second, with its focus on philanthropy it is rooted in the 'how the money is spent' logic that fails to address how CSR shall be implemented into core business operations and strategies. Third, due to the focus on legal responsibilities and the associated liability logic, it does not address the idea of social connection needed when conceptualizing CSR for globalized supply chains and production networks. Fourth, with its focus on economic responsibilities it falls short in cases where there is no business case for CSR, a fundamental problem that we will discuss later in this section.

Crane and Matten (2015) have taken these discussions about ethical motives further. They have argued that beyond the feeling of personal responsibility for the right thing to do, businesses also bear an ethical responsibility because they often cause social and environmental problems and hence ought to solve those problems. This, in essence, also reflects Young's social connection logic (Young, 2004). However, while the social connection approach is morally grounded, companies would probably accept this logic because it might either be profitable to ensure a sustainable supply chain, or more likely because they face substantial stakeholder pressure to behave responsibly.

From an ethical point of view, firms are also embedded in society and thus depend on the contribution of many stakeholders (e.g. employees, suppliers, consumers) and not just shareholders to run their business. Therefore, they have a moral duty to consider the interests and goals of these stakeholders. Next, businesses, in particular large firms, are powerful social actors who have access to substantial resources, so that they ought to use their power and resources responsibly in society. For instance, some of the world's largest firms such as Microsoft, Walmart, Toyota or Volkswagen (and more and more tech firms as well as Chinese corporations) now have revenues higher than the gross domestic product of many countries, justifying the argument that with greater power comes greater responsibility.

Beyond the power argument, because all business activity has some sort of societal (social, environmental or ethical) impact, firms ought not to escape responsibility for those impacts, whether they are positive, negative or neutral. Thus, there is a moral responsibility to manage one's externalities – that is, the impacts of economic transactions borne by those other than the parties engaging in the transaction. Business activity commonly leads to a variety of problematic externalities other than through the provision of products and services, the employment of workers, or advertising techniques. Business ethicists therefore attribute a moral responsibility to businesses that emerges due to negative externalities such as pollution, resource depletion or community problems, specifically if these are not adequately dealt with by governments.

In summary, the ethical responsibilities of businesses generally consist of normative guidelines that depict what companies *should* do beyond economic and legal expectations. Discussions in the literature about ethical motives for CSR continue based on diverse perspectives and moral philosophies such as virtue ethics, Kantian duty ethics, or Rawlsian justice theory. However, as we will show, ethics alone is not a very strong motivation for businesses to engage in CSR, and we would find few companies to behave responsibly simply because it is the right thing to do. Rather, other motives that are based on a much stronger business calculus have taken over.

2.2 Instrumental Motives for CSR – The Business Case

The meta-narrative that pervades much of the debate around CSR is encapsulated in the slogan 'doing well by doing good'. The idea is that being socially or environmentally responsible ultimately pays off and thus contributes to the financial bottom line of a firm. There are four basic factors explaining why CSR can enhance long-term revenue and can create a competitive advantage for firms, thus providing an instrumental motive for CSR (for overviews see, for instance, Hawn & Ioannou, 2016; McWilliams & Siegel, 2001; Vishwanathan et al., 2019).

First, with regard to internal audiences, CSR programmes are said to attract talent, increase employee engagement, motivation and satisfaction, and reduce employee retention, all of which would ultimately contribute to job performance and productivity. For instance, CSR is considered to be a key motivator for millennials when considering a place of work. Second, with regard to external audiences, CSR programmes can enhance trust and support of consumers and investors in products and brands. This allows for creating a favourable reputation, increased sales, and the ability to charge a price premium for socially responsible and sustainable products. Third, with regard to operations, CSR programmes can help to reduce costs. For instance, the implementation of eco-efficiency or recycling measures leads to energy savings and reductions in waste and raw materials used. Fourth, CSR can also allow more effective management of environmental and social risks. For instance, voluntarily committing to a CSR initiative, such as the UNGC, may forestall legislation and ensure greater corporate independence from government. In the aftermath of the Rana Plaza factory collapse in 2013 in Bangladesh that we illustrated in Section 1, many Western retailers were met with calls to ensure worker safety and formed self-regulatory industry initiatives that also helped to prevent negative publicity.

Based on the idea that there is a business case for CSR, a myriad of studies has explored the CSR–financial performance link both theoretically (why would CSR pay off?) and empirically (what is the actual contribution of CSR activities to the financial bottom line?). In one of the most influential theoretical approaches to explain the instrumental motive for CSR, McWilliams and Siegel (2001) developed a supply and demand model for CSR. Based on cost–benefit analysis, this model helps managers to determine the optimal level of CSR a firm should supply in order to maximize financial performance while at the same time satisfying stakeholder demands for CSR (e.g. consumers, employees, community, shareholders). The demand for CSR is affected by factors such as the price premium for products with CSR attributes, consumer awareness, preferences and available income. The supply of CSR actions is influenced by higher costs for labour, machinery and other resources such as materials or services that have higher levels of CSR. CSR attributes may include fair-trade produce such as coffee or tea, non-animal-tested cosmetics, pesticide-free cultivation, dolphin-safe tuna and alternative-fuel engines. CSR actions include such things as recycling, pollution abatement, progressive work practices, and support for local social services. Grounded in the resource-based view of the firm, CSR could create a sustainable competitive advantage if these attributes and actions are founded on resources that are valuable, rare, inimitable and non-substitutable (Barney, 1991), as this allows for product differentiation. In sum, McWilliams Siegel (2001) suggest that managers should treat decisions regarding CSR precisely as they treat all other investment decisions.

Another influential argument for the instrumental motive for CSR has been developed by Jensen (2002) and his idea of 'enlightened self-interest', where businesses take on social responsibilities insofar as doing so promotes their own self-interest. Grounded in neoclassical economics, Jensen proposes that the best strategy to advance social welfare is to maximize the long-term value of the firm. CSR, then, becomes instrumental under the condition that it does not impair the primary corporate objective of maximizing profits. Importantly, as many scholars have criticized, this rather opportunistic view of CSR is the underlying ideology that most advocates of the instrumental perspective seem to accept (see for instance Margolis & Walsh, 2003; Scherer & Palazzo, 2007; Vogel, 2005).

Translating these theoretical approaches into the language of practitioners, Porter and Kramer (2006; 2011) developed the idea of 'Creating Shared Value' (CSV) as one of the most prominent, and more practically embedded, examples of the instrumental view on CSR. Their idea of CSV has been picked up by many businesses around the world as a way to address CSR strategically. This is done by elevating social issues to a strategic level and turning attention away from generic social issues that are not significantly affected by a company's operations nor materially affect its long-term competitiveness. Rather, companies should focus on value chain social impacts. Social issues are thereby significantly affected by a company's activities in the ordinary course of business. Furthermore, main attention should go to the social dimensions of a firm's competitive context, namely those social issues in the external environment that significantly affect the underlying drivers of a company's competitiveness in the locations where it operates. The idea behind CSV is then to prioritize certain social issues along the value chain and transform those social problems relevant to the corporation into business opportunities. Thus, CSV is said to solve societal challenges while simultaneously driving greater profitability, creating so-called win–win scenarios where both a firm and society benefit. While CSV continues to be a popular approach to address CSR strategically, it has also sparked quite a bit of critique, which we will discuss further down.

The relationship between CSR and financial performance has also led to a vast number of empirical studies on the correlation between CSR activities and financial performance (meta-analyses include Orlitzky et al., 2003; Wang et al., 2016). Some have called such correlation the 'holy grail' of CSR research (Devinney, 2009). Findings of more than 150 studies, however, remain inconsistent. Some have found a linear positive relationship where CSR is seen as a business opportunity allowing companies to sell more products or to save costs. Others have found a linear negative relationship where CSR is mainly a burden that involves substantial costs that do not necessarily pay off in the long term. Some studies, consistent with the arguments of McWilliams and Siegel (2001), have found a U-shaped relationship, indicating an optimal level of CSR from a financial point of view. According to that model, firms would be well advised to neither under- nor overinvest in CSR. Lastly, and in contrast to the previous finding, research also discovered an 'inverted' U-shaped relationship. Here, the implication is that the highest payoff from CSR comes from either doing nothing (i.e. avoiding all implementation costs), or addressing CSR substantially and thus reaping the full reputational and other benefits (see Brammer & Millington, 2008).

Due to these inconsistent findings, a clear causal relationship between CSR and financial performance continues to remain an unresolved puzzle. Barnett (2007, p. 794) lamented already more than a decade ago that 'after more than thirty years of research, we cannot clearly conclude whether a one-dollar investment in social initiatives returns more or less than one dollar in benefit to the shareholder'. A possible explanation for this is that significant methodological problems are attached to measuring CSR. We have seen the difficulty in finding a uniform definition of CSR, and its transformation from a philanthropic activity to one that is fundamentally linked to a company's core business strategy. Specifically, meta-analyses suffer from this problem, as they often rely on comparing apples and oranges: some studies link philanthropic expenses to financial performance; others look at reputation rankings or measure more symbolic accounts (such as the existence of a CSR report or code of conduct) rather than substantial CSR actions that are typically more difficult to measure. It thus remains a key problem in this stream of research that studies struggle to measure exactly the same thing (next to adding different mediators and moderators or looking at a different context, industry or firm size). Yet, beyond these methodological problems with the instrumental view on CSR, there are two more important fallacies that we call the 'ethical fallacy' and the 'managerial fallacy' of the business case for CSR.

2.3 Two Fallacies with the Business Case for CSR: Ethical and Managerial Tensions

An important ethical fallacy surrounds the instrumental view on CSR and is reflected in the essential question: if social responsibility is assumed under the condition that it pays off financially, what if it does not pay? The popular concept of CSV that we have introduced provides a case in point where an excessively instrumental focus on the business case for CSR creates a substantial, albeit often overlooked, ethical tension. CSV aims to solve societal challenges by simultaneously driving greater profitability with the creation of 'win–win' scenarios. As Porter and Kramer (2006, p. 6; our emphasis) argue, for CSV, 'the essential test that should guide CSR is *not whether a cause is worthy* [or ethical] but *whether it presents an opportunity to create shared value* – that is, a meaningful benefit for society that is also valuable to the business.' Consequently, 'strategic CSR (i.e., CSV) is far more selective. Companies are called on to address hundreds of social issues, but *only a few present opportunities* to make a real difference to society or to confer a competitive advantage' (Porter & Kramer, 2006, p. 13; our emphasis).

While this, at first sight, sounds too good to be true, it raises a fundamental ethical tension: what if a cause is ethically or socially desirable but does not create added value to the business? What if something is ethically wrong but creates substantial added value to the bottom line? The question that CSV fails to address is what happens when attention to stakeholder interests yields results that diverge from the wealth-maximizing ambitions of a corporation's shareholders. The arguments by Porter and Kramer clearly show that profits come first, and some social benefit second and only if in line with profitability concerns. The ethical fallacy of CSV is thus that it limits ethical behaviour and the acceptance of social responsibility to its value creation potential and not to the solution or avoidance of ethical problems. In consequence, typically only those low-hanging fruits tend to be captured, while the high-hanging fruits we described earlier – cases where it is difficult to establish a business case but which present much more pressing and urgent ethical and societal problems – are ignored.

The logic of the business case approach to CSR, as encapsulated in the idea of CSV, has led to some substantial critique despite the fact that CSV is cherished by many businesses. Crane et al. (2014) for instance have argued that CSV ignores the tensions between social and economic goals, suggesting that it is naïve to assume that win–win situations can easily be established. Rather, drawing on the ambiguous research about the link between CSR and financial performance, they argue that there is 'no evidence that behaving more virtuously makes firms more profitable' (p. 136; citing Vogel, 2005). The fundamental problem is that 'the market for virtue is not sufficiently important to make it in the interest of all firms to behave more responsibly' (ibid.). In other words, while some market participants such as consumers *might* care about CSR and be willing to pay a price premium for it, a large proportion simply does not. In reality ethical tensions are also much more common than win–win situations. CSV thus draws corporate attention to a few best practices and win–win cases and at the same time disguises real problems of systemic injustice such as slave labour in supply chains, massive tax evasion and different forms of inequality.

The instrumental approach to CSR thus carries an important normative deficiency, because it is characterized only by the interests of the most powerful stakeholders of a company, typically shareholders (see Scherer & Palazzo, 2007). The ethical problem is that social responsibility is reduced to another 'success factor', empty of intrinsic value or attention to less powerful stakeholders. Instrumental CSR, in consequence, promotes opportunistic behaviour of businesses where social responsibility is switched on or off, depending on whether there is a business case. Moreover, the approach generally falls short of providing ethically informed guidance for what companies *should* do in sensitive situations where behaving more responsibly does *not* contribute to immediate profitability. The instrumental view on CSR is, however, not only constrained by those ethical tensions as due to the popularity of CSR an important managerial fallacy has also emerged. This fallacy challenges the validity of explanations of CSR behaviour based on instrumental motives.

The managerial fallacy with the business case for CSR, in a nutshell, exists because CSR has transformed from a source of competitive advantage to a competitive necessity. While CSR was at the margins of corporate attention some decades ago, it has become a mainstream concept. Nowadays, almost every larger firm and also many small firms engage in CSR in one way or another (Wickert et al., 2016), often following institutionalized and highly standardized frameworks such as the UNGC or the ISO 26000 implementation scheme (for further information on CSR implementation please see Section 3). Thus, while it might seem like a good idea that 'everybody is doing it', it is precisely the fact that an increasing number of firms follow quite similar paths of action when implementing CSR that complicates instrumental justifications for CSR. In consequence, as the field of CSR matures, the instrumental motive and associated opportunities to create a 'hard' and tangible business case erode and managers face a dilemma: the more societal and competitive pressure there is to engage in CSR, the more difficult it becomes to create a unique CSR profile that allows a firm to 'stand out' and thus generate a sustainable competitive advantage from CSR engagement. Thus, the more firms engage in CSR because they see a business case for it, the more complicated it is to sustain exactly that business case.

A core principle of the resource-based view of the firm indeed suggests that competitive advantage can be created if resources are, among other things, rare, inimitable and unique (see Barney, 1991). Generating such advantage thus works well only if *few* companies do CSR in a *different* manner to create a *distinctive* CSR profile to differentiate themselves from competitors (e.g. offering more sustainable products, treating employees better, etc.). However, what we increasingly see when for instance checking the CSR reports of large multinationals and the portrayal of their CSR strategies on websites, products and services is that they increasingly look alike (think of a green tree in a lush meadow, blue skies and smiling children – a picture that looks fairly familiar when reading across CSR reports). A vast majority of firms includes CSR in their marketing strategy and aims to differentiate their products using CSR attributes such as fair-trade labels, or they position themselves as responsible employers towards job-seekers. The more companies follow a similar approach, the more difficult it would obviously become for a specific firm to be perceived as the most responsible employer if all the competition has pledged for largely comparable or even the same CSR principles, e.g. when they joined the UNGC or report along the same standards of the Global Reporting Initiative (GRI; see Section 3).

Theoretically, these developments mirror a faulty base assumption with regard to CSR being a source of sustainable competitive advantage. Under the conditions of the resource-based view of unique, rare and inimitable resources, CSR can indeed be a valuable element of a product differentiation strategy that may enhance the reputation and/or the brand value of the firm, or pose an entry barrier to competitors. However, companies engaging in a CSR-based strategy can generate financial returns only if they prevent competitors from imitating their strategies. As we have argued, this becomes increasingly difficult the more companies follow standardized CSR templates. At the same time, differentiation by definition implies comparison, such as being a *more responsible* employer, having *more sustainable* products, etc. Thus, what a company does with respect to CSR is more likely evaluated by stakeholders relative to what other firms do and not in isolation or in absolute values. Furthermore, because of its very nature CSR is highly transparent as different societal stakeholders expect to be thoroughly informed about a firm's CSR activities. Banerjee (2008, p. 61) has strikingly summarized the managerial fallacy of the business case for CSR: 'If CSR is indeed a competitive strategy, it is not a particularly valuable one in terms of its imitability: the very visible nature of CSR practices makes it easier for competitors to develop similar strategies.'

The institutionalization of CSR as a corporate 'must-have' is another problem that exacerbates the difficulty of creating a unique CSR profile when everybody is trying to do the same thing in light of the problematic assumptions of the resource-based view of the firm. This, we argue, has become the most important motive that explains why firms engage in CSR: it is simply considered a necessity, rather than a voluntary act. In other words, companies engage in CSR independent of whether it is perceived to immediately or tangibly contribute to profits. Rather, instead of looking for a business case firms engage in CSR because all or most of the competition does. The evidence for this development is vast. A 2017 KPMG survey[14] about CSR reporting, for instance, states that reporting has become a 'standard practice for large and mid-cap companies around the world', and the question is rather *how* to report, rather than *whether* to report (p. 4). Likewise, self-regulatory initiatives in various industries such as UTZ for chocolate and tea, or FSC for sustainable forestry, are typically described as 'semi-voluntary' and participation has transformed from choice to corporate priority. While there is no factual legal obligation for a firm to join such an initiative, it has become 'quasi-mandated' by public expectations about what is considered legitimate business practice.

Various research supports this argument. For instance, a study on justifications for CSR in the opening statements of sustainability reports (Bitaraf, 2015) found that while justifications that linked to the business case ('we engage in CSR because it enhances our profits') dominated around 2005, justifications that link to relational motives and had been marginal a decade ago now present the key reason companies draw on ('we engage in CSR because our stakeholders expect it'). Over the entire period, ethical motives played only

---

[14] https://assets.kpmg/content/dam/kpmg/xx/pdf/2017/10/kpmg-survey-of-corporate-responsibility-reporting-2017.pdf

a marginal role, in other words hardly any company justified its CSR engagement based on the argument that 'it is the right thing to do'. Flammer's (2013) research on shareholder reactions to environmentally oriented CSR initiatives provides evidence that positive stock-market reactions to CSR initiatives have decreased over time, while the negative reactions to irresponsible behaviour have increased. Her research supports our argument that the more becoming 'green' is institutionalized as the norm, the fewer rewards are granted by shareholders when further CSR initiatives are announced. At the same time, however, firms are more likely punished for not following the norm because there is a greater effect of negative news on the public perception of a firm.

In summary, what we have called the 'managerial fallacy' of the business case for CSR argues that opportunities for differentiation and creating a sustainable competitive advantage become more difficult the more CSR becomes mainstream. Thus, when explaining why companies still engage in CSR – a development that is highly visible in the marketplace – we need to turn to other factors in the institutional environment of business firms that go beyond the instrumental motive for CSR.

2.4 Beyond the Business Case: Expanding the Scope of CSR

While the ethical as well as the managerial fallacy continue to be important challenges for the instrumental approach to CSR, the acceptance of social responsibility has moved from the margins to the mainstream. In consequence, other motives not driven by immediate financial considerations have become more important and need to be considered if we want to fully understand why companies engage in CSR. Next, we will describe these as 'relational' motives for CSR, because they primarily reflect corporate responses to the expectations of various stakeholders with which a firm has a relationship.

To approach this question, we first consider the four quadrants shown in Figure 3 that depict four constellations that are either socially/environmentally beneficial or harmful, and either profitable or not (see Karpoff, 2014). While quadrant one represents the business case approach to CSR, quadrants two and three have become more important in light of increasing expectations of societal stakeholders. They reflect areas where stakeholders expect corporate responses to pressing social, ethical and environmental issues more akin to the high-hanging fruits of CSR. This matrix offers a powerful framework, because it reminds us that a business case for CSR certainly exists *in some cases*. However, it strikingly shows that the instrumental approach to CSR *neglects trade-offs* and is limited to those issues of social and environmental responsibility where shared value can be created. As reflected by quadrants two and

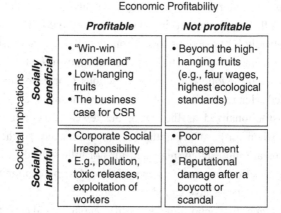

Figure 3: Social implications and economic profitability matrix.
Source: Own illustration after Karpoff (2014).

three, issues where tensions between profits and responsibility arise remain unaddressed in that approach. The matrix thus provides an analytical tool to examine why the 'market for virtue' is not big enough to make it in the interest of all companies to be socially responsible.

Quadrant one marks the CSR territory that is idealized in the instrumental approach to CSR, most prominently by the idea of CSV – a so-called win–win wonderland where societal and business interests are in harmony. *Quadrant two* and *quadrant three* are more challenging and stretch the scope of CSR to more demanding stakeholder expectations. Quadrant two describes a constellation where business conduct is not profitable but socially desirable. This would include very high and thus costly environmental standards or wages to factory workers in cases where there is no labour shortage (as is typically the case for most low-skilled labour). These are activities where stakeholders such as NGOs increasingly expect companies to take action. Quadrant three describes those activities that are profitable but not socially desirable. This includes tax evasion, pollution or consumer fraud. Stakeholders typically expect companies to *not* engage in those activities.

Taken together, these two quadrants best reflect what we can understand as the high-hanging fruits of CSR and are exactly those activities for which companies would struggle to establish a business case for CSR. They would be unlikely to engage in those activities without substantial pressure from stakeholders, for instance as manifested in boycotts or campaigns by NGOs, regulatory threat by governments, or divestment by large groups of socially responsible investors. However, as we will explain below, many companies do indeed engage in those activities in different ways and thus their behaviour can be better understood when looking at how exactly stakeholder pressure is exerted on business firms, rather than how their financial calculations are made. We should not forget *quadrant four* which represents activities which are neither profitable nor socially desirable. This is simply very poor management that will not be discussed further. We will now unfold the relational driver for CSR by explaining the expectations from different kinds of stakeholders as well as the emerging institutional infrastructure for CSR in response to which companies increasingly make a strategic decision to engage in CSR.

2.5 Relational Motives for CSR: Responding to Stakeholder and Institutional Expectations

The scope of CSR – in other words which socially, ethically and environmentally sensitive issues move on the agenda of business firms – is increasingly determined by various societal stakeholders. In consequence, CSR activities are less often a result of a firm's own moral or instrumental judgement about a CSR issue, but more often a reaction to the judgement about those issues of other parties that are mostly external to the firm. Evidence of rising stakeholder influence is for instance provided by NGOs and the threat they can impose by product boycotts or campaigns that target specific companies or industries. A well-known case in point is the cooperation between toy manufacturer LEGO and the oil company Shell. Part of the partnership was that LEGO sold a construction kit that allowed children to build a miniature oil platform. The NGO Greenpeace then launched a campaign urging LEGO to terminate the partnership due to Shell's unsustainable operations in oil exploration and pollution of the Arctic. In fear of negative publicity, LEGO decided to end the sales of the kit. In a similar case, Greenpeace initiated a successful campaign to 'detox' textiles from hazardous chemicals in response to which companies such as Adidas and Puma decided to redesign their products. While the exact scope and content of those campaigns may be contestable, they nevertheless show that companies increasingly react to the expectations of stakeholders and that the threat of a consumer boycott is a serious issue, specifically for firms with well-established brand names.

Stakeholder theory (e.g. Freeman, 1984; Freeman et al., 2018[15]) details who those stakeholders are and what their most important expectations and ways of influencing business firms are. Conceptually, stakeholders are actors who are

---

[15] While in this *Cambridge Element* the notion of stakeholders marks an important part of the CSR discussion, we suggest the *Cambridge Element* on *Stakeholder Theory: Concepts and Strategies* by Freeman et al. (2018) as further reading.

affected by or can affect a business's actions, objectives and operations, independent of whether they have a legal relationship or not. Stakeholders vary in their degree of power and the issues they raise may have different degrees of urgency as well as legitimacy (Mitchell et al., 1997; Section 3 provides further information on assessing stakeholder importance). With respect to CSR, consumers are a key stakeholder group. The demand for fair-trade products for instance has been growing above average over the last decade and now comprises around €8bn globally.[16] Most prominent product categories with a fair-trade certification are coffee, tea, chocolate and forestry products (Lester et al., 2013). While in many categories the share of certified ethical or fair products is still small, more and more companies are entering this market, and perceptions of consumers about the CSR profile has become a strategically relevant concern for most firms, specifically those with valuable reputations.

NGOs, activists and civil society groups are another influential stakeholder group that shapes corporate responses to social issues. As shown by the examples above, NGOs typically stand for a certain environmental or social cause they seek to promote, such as environmental protection (e.g. Greenpeace) or human rights (e.g. Amnesty International). Some NGOs decide to work together with companies and engage in strategic partnerships. The WWF is a prominent example as it has been collaborating with firms like Toyota, Coca-Cola and IKEA to advance environmental protection.[17] Other NGOs deliberately decide to take a more oppositional stance towards the corporate world and focus on launching strategic campaigns to 'name and shame' particularly severe types of wrongdoing such as the well-known campaigns by Greenpeace against Shell or Nestlé. Both types are important in shaping firms' CSR profiles.

Governments and regulatory authorities continue to be relevant stakeholders in the CSR landscape. An important reason for companies to engage in CSR is to anticipate and prevent future regulation. Typically, businesses prefer so-called soft law that is based on voluntary commitments and industry self-regulation over hard law. This is because hard law is in most cases stricter and raises the bar for instance with respect to environmental standards or pollution control. While we have discussed the difficulties of regulating CSR issues on the global marketplace, there has recently been a resurgence of new governmental laws and regulations that specifically address CSR, such as the EU directive on non-financial reporting or US regulations against corruption (Kourula et al., 2019). Thus, an important motive for business firms to engage in CSR is not only to prevent future and typically stricter regulation, but also to

---

[16] www.statista.com/statistics/271354/revenue-of-fair-trade-products-worldwide-since-2004/
[17] https://wwf.panda.org/get_involved/partner_with_wwf/business_partnerships/

simply respond to those new regulations that require for instance the publication of a yearly non-financial report.

Socially responsible investors represent another growing stakeholder group. In the USA for example, the number of investment funds that explicitly include the consideration of social and environmental factors in their investment decisions has more than quadrupled in the last decade, and net assets under management by Socially Responsible Investing (SRI) funds are now more than €4trn.[18] Surveys among millennials support this trend, where according to a poll from 2014 more than half of the population considers social factors when making investment decisions.[19] Even leading wealth managers such as BlackRock put CSR on their agenda, thus urging companies to address CSR if they want to be an investment of choice.[20]

Employees have, similar to consumers, expectations towards companies to be socially responsible and firms react by positioning themselves as attractive employers that pay high attention to CSR. Next to those influential groups, buyers, suppliers and competitors also exert pressure if they source for instance only from companies with strong CSR commitments, avoid being excluded from tenders when not meeting those commitments, or simply seek to not fall behind their peers. Collectively, a so-called institutional infrastructure for CSR has emerged (Waddock, 2008) which comprises the different stakeholders and their interests in furthering some social or environmental concern. Next to those stakeholders we have reviewed, CSR service providers are also important in urging firms to engage in CSR. This includes providers of CSR standards such as ISO 26000, the GRI, other certification bodies that sell their labels such as the FSC or UTZ, as well as many firms that offer CSR consulting or auditing services and obviously too have a financial interest in mainstreaming CSR.

More generally, what this shows is that companies aim to maintain their social licence to operate by acting in accordance with the various expectations of their stakeholders that define the 'rules of the game' and comprise broader societal expectations about what socially responsible business conduct entails. In this context, companies have developed different frameworks and strategies to engage with their stakeholders. We will discuss this in Section 3. In that section, we will also show that in a globalized society, this poses additional challenges as stakeholder expectations are not necessarily consistent and sometimes even ethically questionable. What corporate responses to stakeholder expectations nevertheless have in common is that the underlying rationale is

---

[18] www.eurosif.org/wp-content/uploads/2018/11/European-SRI-2018-Study-LR.pdf

[19] www.investopedia.com/articles/financial-advisors/111315/socially-responsible-investing-how-millennials-are-driving-it.asp

[20] www.nytimes.com/2018/01/15/business/dealbook/blackrock-laurence-fink-letter.html

difficult to quantify or measure in terms of immediate or expected pay-offs. Evidence which shows that companies react to various stakeholder concerns is vast – purely instrumental considerations and a clear business case for these responses are, however, complicated to specify. This is why the relational stakeholder-driven motive for CSR represents a 'soft' business case at best.

Institutional theory offers an important framework to explain these developments, because it examines the processes by which normative and regulative structures such as rules, norms, values and routines become established in society as authoritative guidelines for social behaviour. Research based on this perspective emphasizes that an important premise of institutional theory is imitation: Actors often do not necessarily optimize their structures, practices and decisions, but look at their peers for cues to appropriate behaviour (Marquis & Tilcsik, 2016).

Based on this theory, Campbell (2007) has written a seminal study that provides a comprehensive account of the interplay of various relational motives for CSR which are all linked to the influence of different stakeholder groups and how those groups can push business firms towards accepting greater responsibility. The question asked in the study, 'why would corporations behave in socially responsible ways?', offers an institutional theory of the determinants of CSR, based on the assumption that corporations are embedded in a broad set of economic, political and social institutions that affect their behaviour, and which mainly reflect forces operating outside the immediate boundaries of a firm at the macro- and interorganizational level. Campbell develops a set of eight propositions that reflect economic and institutional conditions which make it more likely that a firm will engage in CSR.

First, he argues that corporations will be less likely to act in socially responsible ways when they are experiencing relatively weak financial performance and when they are operating in a relatively unhealthy economic environment where the possibility of near-term profitability is limited. This, in essence, reflects the assumption that CSR is more likely to incur costs than benefits, and only financially healthy firms can afford to engage in CSR.

Second, corporations will be less likely to act in socially responsible ways if there is either too much or too little competition. That is, the relationship between competition and socially responsible corporate behaviour will be curvilinear. It means that the reputational effect from CSR is strong under 'normal' competitive conditions. In a monopoly, a firm does not need to spend money on costly CSR attributes, as consumers have little choice but to buy its product or service anyway. Under extremely competitive conditions, margins are so low that CSR attributes are simply too expensive to be added onto product features.

Third, corporations will be more likely to act in socially responsible ways if there are strong and well-enforced state regulations in place to ensure such behaviour. This particularly applies to cases where the process by which these regulations and enforcement capacities were developed was based on negotiation and consensus building among corporations, government and the other relevant stakeholders. While empirical evidence on the exact impact of each of those contextual pressures is hard to quantify, the effect of regulatory threat is probably one of the key motives why companies engage in CSR.

Fourth, corporations will be more likely to act in socially responsible ways if there is a system of well-organized and effective industrial self-regulation in place to ensure such behaviour, particularly if it is based on the perceived threat of state intervention or broader industrial crisis and if the state provides support for this form of industrial governance. This proposition complements the previous one and the importance of governmental intervention. It also shows how peer pressure among competitors is an important driver for CSR.

Fifth, corporations will be more likely to act in socially responsible ways if there are private, independent organizations, including NGOs, social movement organizations, institutional investors and the press, in their environment who monitor their behaviour and, when necessary, mobilize to change it. Importantly, this proposition emphasizes that active civil society involvement is critical to advance CSR, including the role of a public watchdog (media), naming and shaming (critical NGOs as for example Greenpeace) and collaboration (NGOs such as WWF).

Sixth, corporations will be more likely to act in socially responsible ways if they operate in an environment where normative calls for such behaviour are institutionalized in, for example, important business publications, business school curricula and other educational venues in which corporate managers participate. Here, the role of proactive education and inclusion of CSR or sustainability courses especially in business schools is highlighted in raising awareness among future leaders.

Seventh, corporations will be more likely to act in socially responsible ways if they belong to trade or employer associations, but only if these associations are organized in ways that promote socially responsible behaviour. Similar to proposition four, effective support structures in the institutional environment of business firms are important to trigger corporate self-regulation, such as pressure exerted by labour unions that represent the interests of employees.

Eighth and finally, corporations will be more likely to act in socially responsible ways if they are engaged in institutionalized dialogue with unions, employees, community groups, investors and other stakeholders. Again, the critical role of the institutional infrastructure for CSR is emphasized, as this allows for knowledge transfer, best-practice sharing and collaboration.

Another important institutionally oriented explanation for why mainstream CSR activities increasingly look alike is that of isomorphism, developed by DiMaggio and Powell (1983). Research on CSR has indeed found that isomorphism increases the more CSR matures and becomes a taken-for-granted practice that businesses are expected to demonstrate – developments that we can readily observe empirically (e.g. Dowell & Muthulingam, 2017; Marquis & Tilcsik, 2016; Shabana et al., 2017). According to this theory, there are three types of isomorphism which, in different ways, make the way CSR is practised increasingly similar. The concept of coercive isomorphism reflects 'forced' adaptation because of formal laws and regulations. It is thus about political pressure and regulatory threat that drive companies to engage in CSR, obviously in similar ways when following the same legislation. For instance, the EU directive on non-financial reporting[21] requires large companies to publish regular reports on the social and environmental impacts of their activities. While the directive allows for some degree of flexibility, it suggests a set of frameworks on how to prepare a CSR report. Such frameworks are the ISO 26000 and the GRI standard which have both become widely accepted standards for reporting contents and formats.

The second type, normative isomorphism, suggests that CSR activities would increasingly look alike because companies tend to follow those norms and values exerted by societal pressures that are considered appropriate. While contextual differences linked to industry or geography certainly exist, many global CSR initiatives have emerged that provide such norms. The UNGC for instance presents itself as a 'moral compass' for responsible behaviour, and its principles are developed to be universally applicable across the globe.

While companies certainly have some leeway in the exact specification of their report and CSR strategies more generally, the concept of mimetic isomorphism also suggests that it is quite likely that their CSR activities would look quite alike. This is because in response to uncertainty about how such things might be perceived by stakeholders, companies adapt mainstream 'best' practices to reduce the risk of deviation from expectations about what proper engagement in CSR would entail. This type of isomorphism, research has found, becomes particularly salient the more CSR matures and becomes a de facto standard. For instance, Shabana and colleagues (2017, p. 1124) who studied sustainability reporting practices found that as CSR matures, the 'cost

---

[21] https://ec.europa.eu/info/business-economy-euro/company-reporting-and-auditing/company-reporting/non-financial-reporting_en

of not participating in CSR reporting becomes so great that CSR reporting makes sense for firms that do not have specific reasons to publish other than the fact that CSR reporting has become the norm'. An increasing number of companies would hence produce a CSR report simply based on the concern that not doing so would reflect badly on them.

In summary, in this section we have examined three important drivers for CSR: ethical, instrumental and relational. Each of them explains why companies would be motivated to engage in CSR, but is based on different rationales. We have argued that the ethical driver plays a rather marginal role and the instrumental one is in decline. At the same time, we have provided evidence suggesting that companies increasingly engage in CSR for relational reasons. Research allows further nuance of this understanding. On the one hand, studies show that among most firms, all three motives coexist, but do indeed have different degrees of salience. For example, Wickert and de Bakker (2018) show that a company's different departments and other internal stakeholders such as engineers, accountants, blue-collar workers or top-managers react differently to those motives. Managers with a business background for instance are more likely to be motivated by the business case for CSR. Blue-collar workers in turn, the study found, are more receptive to ethical motives, i.e. to the 'right thing to do'. Top-managers, in turn, specifically consider relational motives such as the long-term reputation of the firm and its standing with respect to the competition. Other contextual factors are also important. For example, research on small businesses and family firms (e.g. Berrone et al., 2010; Wickert, 2016) shows that many owner-managers care less about profit motives but more about their personal values and sense of ethics when they decide to engage in CSR.

Once we have clarified the reasons why firms would engage in CSR in the first place, the important question emerges: how do business firms implement CSR in organizational practices and procedures? We will unfold this question in the next section.

3 How to Implement Corporate Social Responsibility? Practices, Procedures and the Role of Internal Change Agents

The objectives of this section are:

- To understand how business firms implement CSR principles in internal practices and procedures and become familiar with the most common frameworks used to manage the implementation process.
- To critically examine the role of management tools such as an organization's vision and mission, codes of conduct and CSR policies for transforming CSR intentions into actual practice.

- To acknowledge the difficulties that confront organizations when they aim to create momentum for CSR internally, and to learn about the roles and responsibilities of CSR managers and departments, CSR reporting guidelines and stakeholder engagement strategies.

3.1 From Principles to Actions: What Does the UN Global Compact Suggest?

The UNGC[22] is a case in point to structure the discussion of how companies actually implement CSR. The UNGC provides a hands-on guideline for organizational learning, the so-called *Global Compact Management Model*, which enables firms to recognize and then translate CSR issues into organizational practices. It is based on the UNGC's ten guiding principles on human rights, labour norms, the environment and anti-corruption and includes a sequence of six steps that suggest what companies should do for the transition from broad commitments to the development of a clear CSR strategy and the communication of their progress to stakeholders. The first step is to *commit*. This involves leadership commitment and a clear statement of values that lay the foundation for mainstreaming those values into corporate strategies, policies and procedures and to take measures that support broader goals and issues related to CSR in a transparent way. The second step is to *assess*. This includes assessing risks, opportunities and impacts along the supply chain related to different CSR issues to which a company is connected. The third step is to *define*. This means formulating objectives, strategies and policies that are in accord with the previously assessed risks, opportunities and impacts. Fourthly, there is the need to *implement*. This encompasses the implementation of strategies and policies throughout the organization and its entire value chain. The fifth step is to *measure*. The focus is on determining and monitoring impacts and progress towards the previously defined goals along relevant indicators. Finally, a company needs to *communicate*. This means to report progress and simultaneously engage with stakeholders for continuous improvement. In this section, we will unfold the steps of this general framework for CSR implementation and discuss each in greater detail.

3.2 Realizing CSR Commitments: Value Statements and Codes of Conduct

As highlighted by the framework, the prerequisite for implementation is a commitment to core values and the associated creation of a corporate culture

---

[22] The UNGC and the ten principles have been introduced in Section 1; see www .unglobalcompact.org

that is appreciative of accepting certain social and environmental responsibilities. Such values are typically made explicit in a corporate vision and mission statement. While a vision informs about the desirable goals and future prospects of a firm, the mission contains information on the firm's self-conception and idea where value is added and in which form. Such an idea may link a firm's activity on the market to different societal needs. The vision of the British–Dutch multinational oil and gas company Royal Dutch Shell for example emphasizes its role beyond the pursuit of core business interests, i.e. the extraction and sale of fossil resources, but rather in enhancing the security of supply and energy efficiency and in promoting research, development and introduction of alternative fuels and to drive technology.[23] Hence, one might say that Shell's maxim is as follows: 'We supply energy in the most sustainable way as possible' instead of 'we sell petroleum'. Whether such statements are credible and to what extent they are actually measurable in order to hold companies accountable against their values rests in the eye of the beholder, but it is a matter of fact that companies increasingly include links to sustainability in their values statements in one way or another.

While 'serious' values statements would provide a clear reference point to examine a firm's responsible behaviour, formulating a values statement that emphasizes social responsibility may also encounter ethical problems, specifically in controversial industries. This applies to firms which engage in markets that inevitably contradict with the fulfilment of certain societal needs, for instance, with human rights. The case of the company Lockheed Martin elucidates this. In its values statement, it states that ethics is 'the essence of our business', and goes on to say that:

> *We are committed to the highest standards of ethical conduct in all that we do. We believe that honesty and integrity engender trust, which is the cornerstone of our business. We abide by the laws of the United States and other countries in which we do business, we strive to be good citizens and we take responsibility for our actions.*[24]

However, whether such well-meant intentions are realizable is questionable. In fact, Lockheed Martin's core business is to produce weapons of mass destruction such as nuclear bombs for the US Army. Even if the company might be able to produce weapons in a 'responsible' manner (e.g. under fair labour conditions and with attention to high environmental standards), how 'consumers' use its products in armed conflicts is outside of its influence. Hence, the MNC is not

---

[23] www.shell.com/sustainability/sustainability-reporting-and-performance-data/sustainability-reports.html

[24] www.lockheedmartin.ca/ca/who-we-are/ethics.html

actually able to assure responsibility for its actions. This also explains why many socially responsible investors strictly exclude the weapon industry from their portfolios (Risi, 2018).

More generally, the example raises a critical and still contested tension in CSR, namely that of *process vs. product* responsibility. One may argue that the only thing a company can ensure is a responsible process where the highest CSR standards are upheld. However, one might also claim that whether a company is responsible depends on the product or service it offers (e.g. weapons vs. healthy food). Although, the most sustainable product might be produced under inhumane or environmentally harmful conditions. Thus, while this issue remains contested in the literature, we argue here that full responsibility can be claimed only if attention is paid to both the process dimension of CSR (how are things produced?) and the product dimension (what is actually produced and how could it be used and by whom?).

While values display a company's fundamental principles and self-conception, the *code of conduct*, also known as code of ethics or code of business principles, specifies the measures to implement them and communicates values and norms that guide individual and corporate behaviour. Crane and Matten (2015, p. 190) define a code of conduct as 'a voluntary statement that commits an organization, and industry, or profession to specific beliefs, values, and actions and/or that set out appropriate ethical behaviour for employees [and managers]'. These principles, values, standards or rules of behaviour are thus aimed to facilitate and direct decisions, and formal as well as informal procedures and systems of a business firm. While the code of conduct is thus mainly conceptualized as a guideline for employees, it similarly addresses internal as well as external stakeholders and thus provides the basis for having a dialogue with different stakeholders of the firm.

Almost any larger company nowadays has a code of conduct. Their broad distribution can be explained by the fact that codes of conduct are widely considered as an effective tool to manage CSR. They are commonly an integral part of compliance-based ethics programmes that aim to ensure that laws and corporate standards are fulfilled (Paine, 1994). The German integrated technology company Siemens with business activities in energy, healthcare, industry, and infrastructure and cities, provides a case in point for the importance of codes of conduct. In 2006, Siemens committed a violation of competition law and systematic fraud that resulted in a substantive monetary fine and a severely damaged reputation. Two years after this incident, Siemens launched an extensive compliance-based ethics programme. The aim of the managing board was to develop very strict measures to prevent such incidents being repeated. A core element of the programme was a new code of conduct entitled Siemens

Business Conduct Guidelines, first published in 2009 (Risi, 2013). In the fore-word the then-president and CEO Peter Loescher described the guidelines as the ethical and legal framework within which the company can maintain its successful activities. Furthermore, he mentions that the guidelines prescribe the fundamental principles and rules for the conduct in the firm and in relation to external business partners and the general public. The guidelines are consistent with the law and international conventions and recommendations in the areas of human rights, anti-corruption and sustainability and broadly reflect the ten principles of the UNGC.

Codes of conduct thus specify the measures to implement and communicate those values and norms that a business aims to uphold. Indeed, issues commonly addressed in codes of conduct are labour standards, environmental stewardship and consumer protection. Research also shows that effective codes strike a balance between being a general statement of values and principles that provide a framework of meaning and purpose, and providing practical guidelines for behaviour of managers and employees, for instance in situations such as accepting gifts and how to treat customers (Crane & Matten, 2010, p. 196). In its Code of Business Principles,[25] the Dutch MNC Unilever for example commits to 'conduct our operations with honesty, integrity, and openness, and with respect for the human rights and interests of our employees', and that it is 'committed to safe and healthy working conditions for all employees. We will not use any form of forced, compulsory or child labour.' While these are indeed fairly broad statements, the Code also includes more specific guidelines such as a commitment to 'not give or receive, whether directly or indirectly, bribes or other improper advantages or financial gain. No employee may offer, give or receive any gift or payment which is a bribe.' Several further issues areas are covered and make explicit what employees 'must' and 'must not' do.

3.3 Defining the CSR Pathway: From Codes to Policies for Action

Unilever's Code then makes an important further statement, namely that it and 'the policies that support it … set out the standards required from all our employees. Unilever also requires its third-party business partners to adhere to business principles consistent with our own. These expectations are set out in Unilever's Responsible Sourcing Policy and Responsible Business Partner Policy, which underpin our third-party compliance programme.'

Indeed, many companies have developed *CSR policies* which take those broader commitments outlined in codes of conduct a step further and outline

---

[25] www.unilever.com/Images/code-of-business-principles-and-code-policies_tcm244-409220_en
.pdf

concrete pathways for action on CSR. Many firms for example have an environmental policy, a supplier policy and a human rights policy. To be effective, CSR policies need to be internally embedded and be part of employee training and performance evaluation. Policies often include binding statements and tend to have more strategic weight than a code.

For example, the Dutch multinational banking and financial services company Rabobank has a portfolio of CSR policies called Rabobank Sustainability Policy Framework[26] which aims at implementing the company's sustainability ambitions. These ambitions involve two aspects in particular: on the one hand, Rabobank aims at supporting its clients to realize their efforts for sustainability in and for society. On the other hand, the bank promotes investing in businesses that are forerunners in the area of sustainability. The Rabobank Sustainability Policy Framework comprises the following CSR policies: first, the *Sustainable Development Policy* is an overall policy that comprises all of Rabobank's other sustainability policies and applies to every product and service. Second, *core policies* set expectations related to core environmental, social and governance issues along the UNGC principles and apply to every product and service. Third, *theme policies* refer to thematic issues that are regarded as material for the business, such as biodiversity and animal welfare. Fourth, *sector policies* provide behavioural guidelines for socially and environmentally sensitive industries and supply chains, such as extractive industries, the armaments industry and palm oil. After all, the company's CSR policy seems to have proven of value for implementing Rabobank's sustainability ambitions since the bank has received a number of CSR awards in the past years and appears in a number of sustainability rankings.[27]

While both codes of conduct and policy documents are important starting points for the CSR journey, as we will discuss next, many companies struggle to move from generic commitments, the prioritization of issues and definition of goals, strategies and policies towards real action and the actual implementation of practices that lead to socially and environmentally responsible behaviour.

Indeed, in many cases organizations face many difficulties when attempting to transform their good intentions into substantive action. In fact, the UNGC's Progress Report 2018[28] provides remarkable evidence concerning the gap between

[26] www.rabobank.com/en/about-rabobank/in-society/sustainability/vision-and-policy/vision-sustainably-successful-together.html
[27] www.rabobank.com/en/investors/rankings-awards/index.html
[28] www.unglobalcompact.org/docs/publications/UN-Global-Compact-Progress-Report-2018.pdf

policies and actions that continues to be representative of many MNCs: more than 90 per cent of companies claim to have policies or practices in place that reflect their commitments to the ten principles, while in 68 per cent of companies this is evaluated at the CEO level. Strikingly, these figures diverge substantially when looking at how the same firms integrate CSR into core business strategies and operations. Only 44 per cent of companies report that they move beyond those commitments by integrating responsibility for different CSR aspects into corporate functions and allocating responsibility for the execution of CSR commitments to business units – something that is critical for the substantive implementation of CSR (Risi & Wickert, 2017). More alarming, however, is that this figure decreased from 49 per cent in 2011. The report (p. 19) further highlights that despite very high commitment rates when 'looking at impact assessment, however, we still see a low percentage of companies with a clear assessment of impact'. For human rights for instance, the rates are up a mere 3 per cent from 13 per cent in 2012 to 16 per cent in 2018, while for labour and anti-corruption measures it is similarly low. What should be noted is that these figures are self-assessments by companies and thus likely subject to so-called social desirability response effects where surveys are commonly answered such that they reflect what seems to be an expected or adequate behaviour, rather than what is true. More neutral studies hence arrive at even more alarming conclusions than the UNGC itself (e.g. Berliner & Prakash, 2015; Marquis et al., 2016; Tashman et al., 2019).

These figures reflect that while businesses face increasing societal pressures to adopt CSR, they may respond to such demands in different ways: at the one extreme, there is *symbolic* implementation where formal CSR commitments do not affect daily operations and thus remain decoupled from core business operations. At the other extreme, there is *substantive* CSR implementation where formal CSR commitments are embedded in daily routines and have a significant effect on core business operations. Particularly the latter type of response requires substantial organizational efforts and resources to realize the translation of CSR into corporate practices and processes (Marquis & Qian, 2014; Risi, 2016; Wickert et al., 2016; Wickert & de Bakker, 2018). While we will discuss the problem of decoupling and 'greenwashing' in the next section, we now illustrate the process of substantive CSR implementation and associated difficulties that many companies face along this journey.

3.4 Frameworks for the Systematic Implementation of CSR

CSR management frameworks are widely used tools to help transform good intentions into actual corporate practice and further specify the different steps of the UNGC Management Model. Such frameworks typically depict ideal practices that companies *should* incorporate, given the assumption that they aim to engage in CSR substantively. A vast majority of approaches has been developed by companies themselves, consulting firms, or other stakeholders. While differences exist, most frameworks rest on the following pillars:

- A strong *CSR commitment* clearly informs about how a company's actions relate to CSR. It is about linking respective commitments to measures taken inside a company. Furthermore, a valid CSR commitment elucidates how the company complies with its intentions along the value chain. Commitments are typically incorporated into a code of conduct or policy documents that we discussed above.
- A *CSR strategy* comprehensively addresses how CSR issues are integrated along the management cycle and how CSR links to decision-making on different corporate levels. A CSR strategy brings together a company's different CSR initiatives and programmes in a systematic and coherent manner and thereby reconciles a company's wide range of CSR activities.
- *CSR objectives* explain how a company brings down its intentions to an operational level and translates them into tangible and measurable objectives. In this respect, SMART criteria (i.e. Specific Measurable Accepted Realistic and Timely) are particularly useful for improving target achievement and maintaining it at a high level.
- *CSR measures* aim at integrating CSR objectives into corporate activities. These measures normally take place at the boundaries of a company's operations and may be of various kinds, such as piloting, prevention, corrective measures and capacity building. Furthermore, they may differ with respect to their scope of application, such as corporate departments, supply chain and geographic location.
- *CSR indicators* help to identify performance regarding CSR. A coherent set of indicators allows for measuring a company's CSR in all its facets.
- *CSR monitoring* encompasses procedures of monitoring, auditing and corrective measures. While such procedures help monitor a company's CSR performance, they may differ in terms of frequency, comprehensiveness and scope.
- *CSR achievements* inform about a company's CSR performance in qualitative and/or quantitative terms. Achievements as well as non-achievements are determined based on a company's CSR objectives and indicators. They further allow for building CSR benchmarks in terms of, for instance, comparison with industry norm, regulatory requirements and best practice.

Bondy, Moon and Matten (2012: pp. 288–291) provide an insightful empirical account of how MNCs transform their CSR intentions into action. They mention six phases of CSR implementation where each phase is characterized by distinct patterns of practices. First, firms identify their existing CSR meanings and activities and look into competitor activities. Second, they design the form of their CSR commitments including information on how it will be implemented. Third, firms create and adjust supporting organizational systems and relationships according to their commitments. Fourth, strategy and systems are presented to particular stakeholders and full implementation begins. Fifth, firms communicate CSR performance, and receive and respond to feedback. Sixth, firms revise their strategy and supporting structures based on the feedback from the previous phase.

Others have described CSR implementation from low to high levels of sophistication – or from symbolic to substantive CSR – as a process of organizational learning (e.g. Baumann-Pauly et al., 2013). Zadek (2004) provides an illustrative case of the sportswear and apparel company Nike, which evolved from a negative example to a CSR forerunner through five stages of organizational learning. In the *defensive* stage, a company denies any practices, outcomes or responsibilities with regard to CSR in order to defend attacks that might damage its reputation, and typically has not yet implemented any CSR-related measures ('it's not our job to fix that'). In the *compliance* stage, a company follows a legalistic approach and adopts regulation-based policies in order to avert the erosion of economic value in a mid-term horizon and mainly seeks to meet existing legal obligations ('we'll just do as much as we have to'). In the *managerial* stage, a company begins to integrate social and environmental issues into management processes and everyday business operations, but its approach is rather selective ('we pick the low-hanging fruits'). In the *strategic* stage, a company holistically translates societal issues into core business strategies in order to increase long-term economic value and to secure first-mover advantage ('it gives us a competitive edge'). In the last *civil* stage, a company encourages broad industry participation in CSR also in areas where no legal framework exists and contributes to setting industry standards and self-regulation ('we need to make sure everybody does it and create a level playing-field'). As research shows, not that many companies have reached the strategic or civil stages with respect to the ideal components of CSR frameworks, and a compliance or managerial approach can often be found when looking at those dimensions that go beyond the articulation of a commitment to CSR (e.g. Baumann-Pauly et al., 2013).

While a vast number of CSR implementation frameworks exists, recent attempts have been made to provide a uniform standard and thus comparable approach to implementing CSR. This, as we have outlined in Section 2, is part of the emerging institutional infrastructure for CSR that goes along with

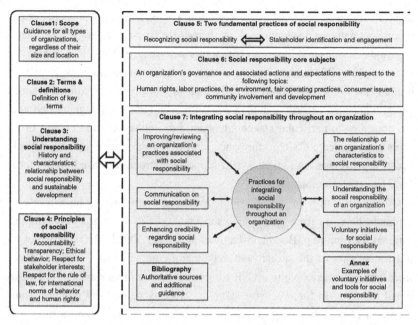

Figure 4: The ISO 26000 CSR implementation framework.
Source: Own adaptation from ISO.[29]

increasing formalization of CSR. A case in point is the so-called ISO 26000 CSR implementation framework that was developed around the year 2010 under the guidance of the ISO, which also provides industry standards on a range of issue areas much beyond CSR (e.g. environmental management, quality, safety, etc.). ISO 26000 provides a blueprint for all types of organizations regardless of their activity, size or location, with the aim of systematically integrating CSR into core business processes. In contrast to other well-known ISO standards, ISO 26000 cannot be certified since it merely provides guidance. However, in close alignment with the principles of the UNGC and the GRI reporting framework, the standard defines what CSR is, supports businesses and organizations in translating principles into actions and shares best practices regarding CSR worldwide.[30] Figure 4 provides a schematic overview of ISO 26000.

On its website,[31] the ISO acknowledges that business firms' 'relationship to the society and environment in which they operate is a critical factor in their ability to continue to operate effectively. It is also increasingly being used as

---

[29] www.iso.org/publication/PUB100260.html

[30] https://www.iso.org/iso-26000-social-responsibility.html

[31] www.iso.org/standard/42546.html

a measure of their overall performance ... ISO 26000 provides guidance on how businesses and organizations can operate in a socially responsible way. This means acting in an ethical and transparent way that contributes to the health and welfare of society.' The guidance that ISO 26000 offers includes the provision of concepts, terms and definitions related to social responsibility; information about the background, trends and characteristics of social responsibility; principles and practices relating to social responsibility; core subjects and issues of social responsibility; pathways for integrating, implementing and promoting socially responsible behaviour throughout the organization and, through its policies and practices, within its sphere of influence; suggestions for identifying and engaging with stakeholders; and guidance for communicating commitments, performance and other information related to social responsibility.

Several clauses complement the standard and specify more precisely what CSR implementation should look like. For example, one clause shows how to gain an understanding of CSR in conceptual and practical terms. This clause also informs about how SMEs may use the standards. Another clause concerns the focus on two CSR practices: how an organization can gain recognition of CSR and how it may conduct stakeholder engagement. This clause provides guidance on the interactions between an organization, stakeholders and society, the recognition of key CSR issues, and on an organization's influence area.

Considering the scope of this and other comparable CSR standards and regional, industry or cultural differences that might lead to prioritizing values differently across contexts shows that the implementation of CSR is a complex endeavour (Risi, 2018). Because of this, business firms have started to professionally address CSR implementation via specified and standalone departments and have been devoting substantial resources to the management of the implementation process. One type of change agent has assumed a focal role in this – the CSR manager.

3.5 CSR Managers as Key Actors Pushing the Implementation

Many MNCs have begun to create dedicated CSR departments and have installed the CSR manager function, i.e. managers who are professionally in charge of developing CSR strategies and managing the organizational integration of CSR (Risi & Wickert, 2017). These managers have become important organizational change agents who play an increasingly important role in creating momentum for sustainability internally. Indeed, according to the Corporate Responsibility Officer Association (recently renamed the Triple Bottom Line

Association),[32] CSR managers are ambassadors, visionaries and strategists who report to the highest executive levels in their companies and serve as champions for CSR who drive commitment within the company and across stakeholders. Wickert and de Bakker (2018), who have studied the work of CSR managers, found that they even consider themselves as 'activists' for social change or like an 'internal NGO' that is responsible for creating more sustainable practices in an organization. Along their journey, however, they oftentimes face considerable resistance among their own employees. This is because substantive integration of CSR typically requires the abandonment of old routines and behaviours and their replacement with more sustainable habits, in other words an oftentimes complete rearrangement of habitualized practices and ways of working. The study[33] found that to overcome such resistance, CSR managers draw on a range of strategies to rally people for CSR.

1. *Building a network of internal allies*: This involves identifying others who share the passion for sustainability and making them 'internal allies' who support the implementation of CSR. Such intra-organizational networks can play an important role in leveraging CSR managers' influence. The strategy is particularly important for initiating pilot CSR projects, such as a corporate recycling programme.

2. *Make sustainability resonate*: CSR managers need to establish a connection between CSR issues and employees and their business routines in order to explain what CSR means in daily practice. This lays the foundation for increasing commitment and supporting employees' identification with relevant CSR aspects.

3. *Identify adequate incentives for CSR*: This strategy supports the establishment of emotional and functional connections by accommodating employees' heterogeneous understandings of what CSR means, why CSR is (or is not) important and therefore what motivates them to engage with CSR.

4. *Benchmarking against internal and external parties*: CSR managers can stimulate internal competition between corporate divisions and external competition with competitors about the 'best' CSR performance. Such a competitive environment helps to motivate all those involved to engage in CSR.

5. *Promoting awareness of CSR*: This activity stimulates independent and proactive recognition of CSR issues in the day-to-day activities of employees and managers from the bottom up.

---

[32] www.3blassociation.com/

[33] https://hbr.org/2019/01/how-csr-managers-can-inspire-other-leaders-to-act-on-sustainability

Research has also aimed to explain the roles and responsibilities of CSR managers from a theoretical point of view. Interestingly, contrary to what might be commonly assumed, the importance of CSR managers in an organization might not necessarily increase the more substantive CSR becomes implemented. Risi and Wickert (2017) found that as CSR becomes institutionalized, CSR managers might become marginalized. This is because of the following reasons: in order to implement CSR throughout an organization, CSR managers carry expert knowledge of CSR (e.g. the issue of health and safety in managing human resources) to employees and managers in other departments in charge of 'executing' the CSR strategy. In consequence, the more CSR managers have conveyed their knowledge and the more is absorbed by relevant other actors in the organization (e.g. procurement or production managers now know how to handle CSR expectations), the more difficult it becomes for CSR managers to still claim their role as key expert in CSR. Thus, the study found that in particular in early phases of the CSR journey, CSR managers have an important 'trigger' function as key carriers of CSR knowledge and are regarded as key change agents. However, they become pushed to less important administrative roles, such as compiling the yearly CSR report, the more the organization progresses to higher levels of implementation. CSR managers are, however, able to counteract their declining importance if they identify new CSR issues and put them on the agenda, such as the recently emerging topic of responsibility related to digitalization.

In a nutshell, CSR implementation corresponds to a dynamic and complex organizational process that involves different areas of a company and is not reducible to the standalone CSR department. Instead, the CSR department and its managers should be regarded as the starting point for the implementation journey. Substantive implementation, however, requires that CSR knowledge, practices and procedures have diffused into all areas and functions of a company. Importantly, this insight challenges the usual criteria applied by rating agencies to assess the degree to which a company has implemented CSR. For instance, companies that install a CSR position in the top management are three times more likely to be included in the Dow Jones Sustainability Index (Strand, 2013). However, as shown above, investing resources into the CSR department does not automatically mean substantive CSR. Instead, while early stages of CSR implementation are characterized by investing more resources in a CSR department, such direct investments into the department decrease as the process of implementation advances (Risi, 2016). Next to driving the internal implementation of CSR, CSR departments typically also have the important function of communicating their actions to external stakeholders.

3.6 CSR Reporting: Communicating Progress to Stakeholders

As the Global Compact Management Model suggests, communicating about the progress made in implementing CSR internally is an important component of a firm's overall CSR engagement and shows that it is indeed 'walking the talk'. This brings us to the issue of CSR reporting. The professional service and audit firm KPMG notes in its 'KPMG Survey of Corporate Responsibility Reporting 2017'[34] that CSR reporting has become a standard practice for large and mid-sized companies around the world. While 78 per cent of the world's biggest companies inform on financial and non-financial data in their annual financial reports, every sector analysed by KPMG has a minimum CSR reporting rate of 60 per cent – the question for companies became indeed *how* to report, not whether to report. Furthermore, the survey indicates that among the world's 250 largest companies the assurance of CSR data has more than doubled in the last twelve years, making it a common expectation that stakeholders have about CSR reports – and a huge business for those firms that offer such assurance. While service providers are part of the influential institutional infrastructure for CSR that we have discussed above, regulatory requirements have also pushed the uptake of CSR reporting and made it a key component of the overall implementation process.

In 2014, the European Commission issued a directive[35] that makes the disclosure of non-financial information and the way companies operate and manage social and environmental challenges mandatory for public-interest companies with more than 500 employees. According to the European Commission, this 'helps investors, consumers, policy makers and other stakeholders to evaluate the non-financial performance of large companies and encourages these companies to develop a responsible approach to business'. Member states were required to transpose this directive into national laws and, against this background, the first wave of mandatory CSR reports concerning the financial year 2017–2018 was published in 2018. The directive is part of the broader EU CSR initiative that aims to promote inclusive and sustainable growth in view of the Europe 2020 objectives and involves consistent CSR reporting.

Under the directive, companies have to publish reports on the strategies, policies and measures they implement in relation to environmental protection, social responsibility and treatment of employees, respect for human rights, anti-corruption and bribery, as well as diversity on company boards (in terms of age, gender, and educational and professional background). In doing so, the directive

---

[34] https://home.kpmg.com/content/dam/kpmg/campaigns/csr/pdf/CSR_Reporting_2017.pdf
[35] https://ec.europa.eu/info/business-economy-euro/company-reporting-and-auditing/company-reporting/non-financial-reporting_en

allows companies some flexibility to disclose relevant information in the way they consider most useful. Companies may use international, European or national guidelines to produce their statements – for instance, they can rely on the UN Global Compact, the OECD guidelines for multinational enterprises, ISO 26000, and the GRI's Sustainability Reporting Guidelines.

In light of this, the GRI standard has become one of the most commonly applied frameworks for CSR reporting. The GRI standard helps businesses, governments and other organizations to understand and communicate their impacts on key CSR issues such as climate change, human rights and corruption. While the link to the ten guiding principles of the UNGC is obvious, both are complementary initiatives that should help organizations regardless of size, location or sector to foster CSR and sustainable development and to transparently report on progress[36]. In general, the aim of the GRI standard is to ensure that a report portrays a balanced and comprehensive image of an organization's economic, environmental and/or social impacts, and consequently how it positively and negatively contributes to sustainable development. According to the GRI, standardized corporate communication allows internal and external stakeholders to gather respective information and make well-founded decisions about an organization's contribution to CSR. At the same time, most CSR communication faces a substantive limitation. Namely, it reflects a rather one-way, 'transmission-oriented' way of communication where information about CSR is directed at stakeholders. However, stakeholders increasingly expect participation in MSIs and thus influence business strategies for CSR, in other words a two-way, 'interaction-oriented' communication style. In consequence, business firms are urged to involve stakeholders and have developed various ways of stakeholder engagement which we discuss next.

3.7 Stakeholder Engagement

Stakeholder engagement is a process by which an organization establishes communication channels with the interest groups in its organizational environment. Stakeholder engagement provides the basis for integrating the different views of interest groups into organizational decision-making and helps an organization to anticipate the impact of its activities on such groups. Stakeholder engagement is considered an important element of CSR. The GRI standard also requires a comprehensive disclosure of an organization's approach to stakeholder engagement. ISO 26000 emphasizes the importance of stakeholder engagement by closely connecting the identification of and engagement with interest groups to the recognition of an organization's key

---

[36] www.globalreporting.org/information/about-gri/alliances-and-synergies/pages/ungc-and-gri.aspx

CSR subjects and issues and its influence area. All of this reflects the political approach to CSR that we discussed in Section 1 and which explicitly calls upon businesses to engage in deliberative processes with stakeholders in order to legitimize their actions.

Freeman (1984), in his elaboration of the stakeholder theory of the firm, suggests that companies have to consider the rights and interests of all stakeholders.[37] More specifically, he suggests that businesses' responsibility lies in acting in the interests of stakeholders, not merely shareholders. In consequence, decision-makers have to deal with a multitude of different stakeholders that have direct relations with the company, such as employees and customers, as well as parties that have only tenuous economic relations, such as politicians and representatives of NGOs. This poses the question of stakeholder prioritization: to whom should we give attention? Based on stakeholder theory, Mitchell, Agle and Wood (1997) provide a useful framework for assessing stakeholder importance. Their framework divides the question as to which stakeholder an organization should pay attention to into three interconnected sub-questions. The first sub-question relates to power, which means that an actor is able to enforce its will even in the case of resistance, and asks: is the stakeholder able to affect the organization? The second sub-question connects to legitimacy, broadly defined as socially accepted and expected behaviours and structures, and asks: how justified is the interest of the stakeholder? The third sub-question concerns urgency, that is, calling for pressing and/or instant attention. The resulting question is: does the stakeholder deserve immediate attention?

Answering these questions allows the classification of stakeholders into different categories of varying importance. Mitchell et al. (1997) suggest that 'definitive' stakeholders that have all three attributes – power, legitimacy and urgency – should be at the centre of attention for a firm, while those that are 'dangerous', 'dominant' and 'dependent' also need to be observed carefully (see Figure 5). Such categorization, in essence, reflects an instrumental view of stakeholders where attention is given only to those who matter financially (Jones, 1995). Business ethicists have criticized this version of stakeholder theory, because a morally legitimate way of engaging with stakeholders would pay equal attention to all stakeholders no matter how powerful they are (Donaldson & Preston, 1995). Notwithstanding these theoretical arguments, the way business firms actually engage with stakeholders and determine the materiality of their claims rather mirrors the instrumental approach.

---

[37] See also the Cambridge Element *Stakeholder Theory: Concepts and Strategies* by Freeman et al., (2018).

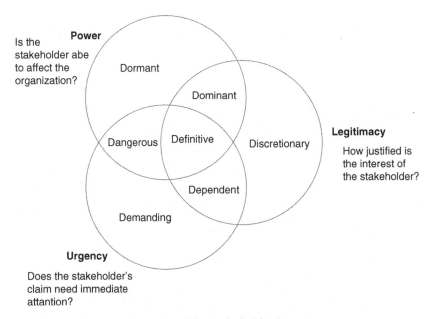

Figure 5: Identifying stakeholder importance.

Source: Mitchel et al. (1997).

The so-called materiality analysis is a widely used management tool for identifying the importance of CSR issues from the perspective of a business and of its stakeholders. Materiality analysis encompasses a field analysis of relevant CSR issues in the firm's environment, an internal analysis of existing practices and procedures, and an analysis of stakeholders and their expectations towards those issues. These analyses converge in a matrix with two dimensions: first, an axis that is typically called 'impact on business success'; second, an axis that is typically called 'importance to stakeholders'. The German reinsurance firm Munich Re for example, as stated on its website,[38] has identified climate change as the key topic that matters both for the company and its stakeholders and thus holds a key place in its CSR strategy. Demographic change, in turn, has been identified by both the company's stakeholders and itself as a topic of low importance. The Dutch MNC Unilever conducts a similar analysis[39] and packaging & waste, for instance, has been identified as one of the most material issues for both the company and its stakeholders. Ideally, these issues then feed back into the overall strategy and corresponding practices.

This type of analysis, as commonly practised by many business firms, seems unproblematic as long as the firm and its stakeholders agree about what is

---

[38] www.munichre.com/corporate-responsibility/en/strategy/stakeholder/index.html
[39] www.unilever.com/sustainable-living/our-approach-to-reporting/defining-our-material-issues/

important and what is not. Complications arise if there is no agreement about some CSR issues that might be material or worthy from a stakeholder point of view, but incorporating them into the CSR strategy would be unlikely to bring the expected payoffs. Crane and Matten (2010) have argued that multiple problems can emerge in stakeholder collaborations which could explain why companies may refrain from engaging too closely with their stakeholders. First, such engagement is time-consuming and expensive and it is difficult to make quick decisions. Second, there is often a culture clash, because companies and stakeholders often exhibit very different values and world views, e.g. critical NGOs like Greenpeace vs. companies in controversial industries such as Shell. Third, and linked to the previous point, is uncontrollability. In other words, there is no guarantee that a mutually acceptable outcome will be reached. In consequence, companies may lose control over their strategic direction. Fourth, co-optation of stakeholder groups has been recognized. For instance, the UNGC has been accused of 'bluewashing' and for being more in favour of corporate rather than societal interests (Berliner & Prakash, 2015). This obviously threatens the credibility of a stakeholder group and its claims. At the same time, however, critical stakeholder groups also need to be held accountable for their actions and expectations. Not necessarily all NGOs and other stakeholder groups have legitimate claims, or they might have claims which are shared only by a particular group (e.g. religious fundamentalists who protest against a company that promotes equal opportunities for LGBTQ people).

3.8 Summary

In this section we have addressed the question of how organizations implement CSR principles in practice. We have introduced the most popular frameworks used for CSR implementation such as the Global Compact Management Model, and discussed the importance of an appropriately formulated corporate vision and mission. We have further argued that implementing CSR is a difficult endeavour which corresponds to an organizational learning process through which organizations go when they develop a sense of CSR. Specific CSR management frameworks, such as ISO 26000, have been presented since they are widely considered useful to initiate and to facilitate such a learning process. We have mentioned the strengths and weaknesses of such frameworks as in the case of the one-size-fits-all ISO 26000 approach. We have then pointed out the trend that many organizations have started to professionally address CSR implementation via standalone CSR departments and the employment of CSR managers as important change agents. We have completed this section by discussing CSR reporting in accordance with the GRI guidelines and the importance of a company's stakeholder engagement. With regard to the latter, we have additionally clarified the issue of stakeholder prioritization and introduced materiality analysis that is widely used in practice for the identification of CSR issues of importance for a company and its stakeholders. We have concluded by mentioning some problems with stakeholder collaboration and interaction. In the next section, we will further focus on the limitations and difficulties of CSR implementation. In this respect, we will elaborate on the issue of so-called greenwashing.

4 The Dark Side of CSR: Greenwashing and Other Forms of Corporate Social Irresponsibility (CSiR)

The objectives of this section are:

- To examine greenwashing as a common phenomenon in the field of CSR and to show how it can be detected in its different forms.
- To understand the theoretical reasons why and under what conditions business firms are likely to exhibit greenwashing behaviour.
- To learn about ways to better distinguish substantive CSR efforts from symbolic impression-management tactics.

In Section 3 we discussed ideal steps and practices required for organizations to substantively implement CSR. At the same time, we made the distinction between *substantive* and *symbolic* CSR implementation. While there are many examples of firms that do take CSR seriously and that undertake substantive efforts to implement socially and environmentally responsible business practices, there is also vast evidence of more symbolic forms of CSR. This phenomenon is commonly known as 'greenwashing' or 'window-dressing'. The Oxford Dictionary[40] defines greenwashing as 'disinformation disseminated by an organization so as to present an environmentally [or socially/ethically] responsible public image'. Another definition suggests that 'greenwashing is the intersection of two firm behaviours: poor environmental performance and positive communication about environmental performance' (Delmas & Burbano, 2011, p. 65). These two definitions capture the essence of greenwashing, which is not simply about irresponsible or environmentally damaging behaviour of firms. On top of that, a greenwashing firm simultaneously presents itself as socially or environmentally responsible so as to construct a 'CSR facade' to deflect public attention away from its wrongdoing. Importantly, while the expression greenwashing was originally linked to environmental issues (hence the colour green), we explicitly include here all those other social

---

[40] https://en.oxforddictionaries.com/definition/greenwash

and ethical issues that commonly fall under the umbrella of CSR. Furthermore, greenwashing can be linked to a specific product as, for example, in case of false advertising. Greenwashing can also apply to a firm more generally when comparing its CSR commitments and impression-management strategy with its broader production processes.

Why is it important to discuss greenwashing in the context of CSR? It is because, on the one hand, we are witnessing an ever-increasing intensification of the discourse about sustainability and CSR. Nearly every firm nowadays has something to say about its CSR efforts, how sustainable its operations are and how well it treats its employees, even in the supply chain. Typical CSR reports of MNCs give the impression that we, put bluntly, don't have to worry about the future of our planet because business is doing so much to make it sustainable for future generations. On the other hand, reports abound that provide alarming evidence of corporate misbehaviour such as pollution, use of toxic materials, human rights abuses, modern slavery, corruption and tax avoidance. It is not uncommon for firms that have the longest and most elaborate sustainability reports, and that receive numerous awards, to face the most severe accusations of Corporate Social Irresponsibility (CSiR). Car manufacturer Volkswagen for instance was industry group leader in the Dow Jones Sustainability Index[41] and was applauded by the rating agency Reputation Institute for its excellent corporate governance practices, including 'a preventive approach to compliance' and a code of conduct that was supposed to ensure ethical behaviour among all employees and members of executive bodies.[42] What followed was one of the largest corporate scandals in German industrial history, namely the massive and systematic cheating of car emissions of its fleet that might even be considered a case of organized crime. What came to be known as Dieselgate not only led to numerous lawsuits, plummeting share prices and billions of euros of 'clean-up' costs, but also a substantial drop in Volkswagen's reputation. What the Volkswagen case demonstrates is that seemingly superior CSR performance often lies alongside irresponsible root structures behind a green CSR facade.

One does not have to look far to find further media coverage about child labour in the textile industry, misleading information about climate science, or consumer deception in product labelling – oftentimes linked to exactly those firms that claim to be CSR leaders. Likewise, macroeconomic figures that cannot be easily attributed to a specific firm, such as climate change and carbon dioxide emissions, waste production and societal health, also cast doubt on whether the aggregate CSR activities of business firms really have an impact on

---

[41] www.robecosam.com/csa/csa-resources/industry-leaders.html

[42] https://cdn2.hubspot.net/hubfs/2963875/Resources/2014%20Global%20CSR%20RepTrak%
20100.pdf?submissionGuid=1a760de1-6a1f-4dc3-a966-a52ff77db94d

the overall state of the natural environment and societal well-being. For example, those countries that often praise themselves as leaders in sustainability and assume a great self-awareness of the need to be responsible score highest in carbon dioxide emissions or disposable plastic usage per capita.[43] A report by Oxfam suggests that the richest 10 per cent of the world's population – including those who lead the discourse about sustainability – are responsible for about half of all carbon dioxide emissions globally, while the poorest 50 per cent – including those who would probably never consider themselves ethical consumers – are responsible for only 10 per cent of all emissions.[44]

In 2013, a Europewide assessment of the actual impacts of CSR activities on the social and environmental fabric of the EU was published.[45] Unsurprisingly perhaps, it found that there is little empirical evidence of any notable impacts of things labelled CSR. The report concludes that the aggregate CSR activities of European companies in the past decade have not made a significant contribution to the achievement of the broader environmental and social policy goals of the EU. Halme and colleagues (2018, p. 2; our emphasis) have similarly questioned why, despite so much research on the business case for CSR (see Section 2), there is as yet little research about what they call a 'sustainability case' – in other words, 'whether and when CSR management contributes to *real* improvements in the environmental and social performance of companies'. This, they argue, is surprising as the very *raison d'être* of CSR should be to respond to societal concerns about the negative environmental and social externalities of business firms.

Critics of CSR have indeed called into question the assumption that CSR activities automatically lead to greater sustainability. Some have even argued that CSR has failed to promote a better society and reduce ecological harm that results from business activity (Banerjee, 2008; Fleming & Jones, 2013). At the same time, a vast number of studies provides evidence and theoretical explanations of corporate greenwashing and the broader question of why many business firms are not walking the talk of CSR (e.g. Bowen, 2014; Delmas & Burbano, 2011; Tashman et al., 2019; Wickert et al., 2016). In this section, we will therefore critically analyse representative cases of greenwashing and discuss some literature that has attempted to explain theoretically why such forms of misbehaviour are so prevalent in the world of business.

4.1 Detecting Greenwashing

Greenwashing can take many forms. Some are obvious to informed consumers, such as simply painting products in green and adding some pictures of nature.

---

[43] https://data.worldbank.org/indicator/EN.ATM.CO2E.PC

[44] www.oxfam.org/en/research/extreme-carbon-inequality

[45] www.abis-global.org/projects/impact; https://cordis.europa.eu/project/rcn/95940/reporting/en

These can often be found on consumer products such as (fast) food, beverages, beauty or electronics, and in many advertisements of those products. Other forms of greenwashing are much subtler and more hidden and they can often be detected only after detailed scrutiny of what a firm does on the 'front stage' compared to what is happening 'backstage'.

Many NGOs have devoted considerable resources to inform consumers about greenwashing. A notable study was published by the US-based NGO Terrachoice,[46] which made an important early move to classify different types of greenwashing, namely by identifying the 'seven sins of greenwashing'. According to this report, 95 per cent of all consumer products in the USA that claim to be green commit at least one of the seven sins (see Table 2). This classification has been an impactful tool that many other activist groups have used in their campaigns against greenwashing. While almost a decade old, a quick internet search suggests that those findings are still valid today.

Greenpeace has also devoted itself to the fight against greenwashing, and has been influential in making the term popular. During the UN conference on sustainable development in Rio de Janeiro in 2012, it published a noteworthy report, 'Greenwash +20',[47] which provides further evidence of corporate mis-behaviour related to the environment. In its investigations about greenwashing, Greenpeace developed the following four criteria: first, greenwashing often occurs in so-called Dirty Businesses, where often trivial environmental pro-grammes or products are being praised while core business operations are inherently polluting or unsustainable. For example, many oil companies such as Shell or BP often applaud their own investments in renewable energy while these remain relatively marginal compared to their investments in polluting practices such as traditional oil extraction. In those firms' PR campaigns, however, clean energies receive an unduly high share of presentation so as to deflect stakeholder attention away from the dirty side of business.

Second, greenwashing is often linked to so-called Ad Blusters, where adver-tising or PR campaigns overstate environmental achievements to divert atten-tion away from more fundamental environmental problems. A somewhat extreme case can be found in the tobacco industry, where Philip Morris spent around US$75m on charity, while at the same time spending around $100m on a marketing campaign to promote its charity engagement (Palazzo & Richter, 2005). Shell provides another illustrative example of Ad Bluster greenwashing. In 2007, the company published an advertisement in newspapers and magazines

---

[46] http://sinsofgreenwashing.com/index35c6.pdf

[47] www.greenpeace.org/archive-international/Global/international/publications/RioPlus20/GreenwashPlus20.pdf

Table 2: The seven sins of greenwashing.

Sin of the hidden trade-off	If a product is branded green based on an unreasonably narrow set of attributes without attention to other important environmental issues. Paper, for example, is not necessarily environmentally preferable just because it comes from a sustainably harvested forest, in that other important environmental issues in the papermaking process, including energy, greenhouse gas emissions, and water and air pollution, may be ignored.
Sin of no proof	If an environmental claim cannot be substantiated by easily accessible supporting information or by a reliable third-party certification. Common examples are tissue products that claim various percentages of post-consumer recycled content without providing any evidence.
Sin of vagueness	If a claim is so poorly defined or broad that its real meaning is likely to be misunderstood by the consumer. 'All-natural' is an example. Arsenic, uranium, mercury and formaldehyde are all naturally occurring, and poisonous. This means that 'all natural' is not necessarily green or sustainable.
Sin of irrelevance	If an environmental claim is truthful but is unimportant or unhelpful for consumers seeking environmentally preferable products. Avoidance of toxic substances in products is a common example, where law in any event bans those substances.
Sin of lesser of two evils	If a claim is true within the product category but distracts consumers from the greater environmental impacts of the category as a whole. Examples of this category might include organic cigarettes or fuel-efficient sport utility vehicles.
Sin of fibbing	If an environmental claim is simply false. The most common examples were products falsely claiming to be energy Star certified or registered.
Sin of worshiping false labels	If a product, through either words or images, gives the impression of third-party endorsement while no such endorsement actually exists; fake labels, in other words.

Source: Terrachoice.

showing flowers coming out of the chimneys of a refinery.[48] Supposedly, so was the argument, the carbon dioxide emissions from that refinery were recycled and

---

[48] www.theguardian.com/media/2007/nov/07/asa.advertising

then used as fertilizers to grow plants. Later that year, the Dutch Advertising Authority instructed Shell to stop misleading the public with this advertisement, after the NGO Friends of the Earth Netherlands filed a complaint. The Advertising Authority confirmed that this was a misrepresentation, since only a tiny proportion of Shell's total carbon dioxide emissions is piped into greenhouses. According to the rule, readers could misinterpret that claim and assume that Shell would use all, or at least the majority, of their waste carbon dioxide to grow flowers, whereas the actual amount was a very small proportion when compared to the global activities of Shell. A campaign leader of Friends of the Earth Netherlands indeed summarized the main critique:[49] 'Instead of greenwashing its environmental behaviour, Shell should tackle its real problems. For instance, in Nigeria, gas flaring by Shell causes 60 times more greenhouse gas emissions than the carbon dioxide that is reused by Dutch farmers to grow flowers.'

Third, Political Spin is a more subtle and hidden form of greenwashing: firms advertise or talk about their CSR commitments while they simultaneously lobby against stricter regulation on the same topic. Many examples stem from the automotive industry. BMW, for instance, has been praising itself as a leader in CSR. In its 'Sustainable Value Report 2017',[50] BMW proclaims that 'The BMW Group is the most successful and sustainable premium provider of individual mobility.' At the same time, however, evidence suggests a more than dubious role of BMW in lobbying the German government and European Commission against stricter environmental regulation. During the 2012 London Olympic Games for example, a report by the newspaper *The Guardian*[51] accused BMW of hypocrisy over its opposition to European carbon emissions targets, most likely because of its strong focus on high-consumption luxury cars. While BMW was said to lobby against tougher emission proposals, it held up its green credentials as a sponsor of the Olympics electric car fleet. The article cites a representative of the campaign group Transport and Environment who stated that 'It is time for the hypocrisy to stop. BMW should stop talking up how green and efficient their cars are while at the same time lobbying to weaken planned regulations to improve the fuel efficiency of cars. Car buyers want more fuel-efficient vehicles, that put money in drivers' pockets through lower fuel bills.'

Fourth, there is greenwashing if pro-environmental or social behaviour is merely reflecting legislation. Indeed, many firms use extensive PR campaigns to

[49] www.foei.org/press/archive-by-subject/resisting-mining-oil-gas-press/shells-advert-misleading
[50] www.bmwgroup.com/content/dam/bmw-group-websites/bmwgroup_com/ir/downloads/en/2017/BMW-Group-SustainableValueReport-2017–EN.pdf
[51] www.theguardian.com/environment/2012/jul/09/bmw-hypocrisy-european-car-targets

advertise or brand products with certain supposedly proactive environmental achievements which are no more than compliance with basic environmental laws. For example, according to research, particularly in the most intensely regulated industries such as oil, gas and minerals extraction, exactly those key players such as Shell, BP, Vale, Rio Tinto and Anglo-American face the most severe greenwashing allegations (Lyon & Montgomery, 2015). In fact, 'companies sometimes position themselves as sustainable and drown the readers of their CSR reports in technical data but do no more than comply with basic environmental laws' (Scherer & Palazzo, 2007, p. 1114).

4.2 Explaining Greenwashing

While the empirical evidence of greenwashing is vast and has been covered in both research and the media, scholars have also aimed to develop theories that help understand the underlying reasons and motives that explain why and under what conditions greenwashing occurs so frequently. Next, we will delve into some of the more prominent attempts.

The notion of decoupling, which stems from institutional theory, has been widely applied to examine the reasons behind greenwashing and symbolic forms of CSR. Already in the 1970s and studying primary education, Stanford-based scholars Meyer and Rowan (1977) suggested that what they labelled as decoupling is about creating and maintaining a gap between symbolically adopted policies and actual organizational practices. This gap is a response to pressures from the institutional environment of an organization to comply with social regulations and norms about how organizations should be structured and operated. Decoupling policy from practice then occurs when an organization on the one hand aims to be perceived as legitimate or responsible by societal stakeholders, and on the other hand faces a need to ensure technical efficiency in internal operations. Scott (2008, p. 171) summarized the essence of decoupling as follows: decoupling 'allows organizations to signal compliance symbolically without changing their practices substantively'. In CSR-terms, this means that a company would use CSR commitments to brand itself as socially responsible in the eyes of its stakeholders and receive favourable evaluations, for example, by investors, while in reality all that is done with respect to those commitments is that they are posted on the corporate website or mentioned in the CEOs' public speeches. In addition, decoupling can be more specific when, for example, a product is marketed as green, while in reality its ingredients or the underlying production processes are not.

Research into CSR has indeed found that building an external appearance or facade of CSR without corresponding substantive internal practices and procedures is often relatively inexpensive and even sufficient to be perceived as socially responsible, at least in the short term and when those internal practices are difficult for external parties to thoroughly evaluate (Christmann & Taylor, 2006; Wickert et al., 2016). However, research also points out that stakeholders penalize greenwashing firms more than those who simply remain silent about their CSR behaviour, even if the former organizations are ecologically friendlier. In other words, CSR communication raises expectations among stakeholders and the wider the gap between proclaimed and actual performance, the greater the penalty. For example, Lyon and Maxwell (2011) show that BP, portraying itself as 'Beyond Petroleum' and a self-proclaimed oil industry leader in the energy transition, has received greater pressure from activists for its environmental record than Exxon, a firm considered as having a worse ecological performance but which at the same time less aggressively communicated its CSR credentials.

In Section 3 we discussed the prevalence of codes of conduct and CSR policies in many businesses that nonetheless often go no further than being a favourable representation of commitments to CSR. Substantive implementation, as for example the UNGC study suggests, often lags behind. Scholars have described the intentional gap between what a firm preaches and what it practises as 'policy–practice decoupling' (e.g. Bromley & Powell, 2012). However, there is also a more complicated form of decoupling, namely means–ends decoupling. Here, formal policies are actually implemented into daily practices, but they fail to achieve the proclaimed outcomes. The widespread development and application of biofuels is a case in point. While many firms should not be accused of greenwashing when they have substantively integrated their biofuels policy and produced engines for this type of fuel, at the macroeconomic level it remains doubtful at best whether those fuels are truly sustainable, for instance, when considering the necessary land use and deforestation involved.

Next to decoupling, researchers have examined other symbolic compliance strategies that help to better understand the reasons behind greenwashing. Marquis and Toffel (2012) for instance argued that 'attention deflection' is a strategy used by businesses to implement alternative and supposedly cheaper practices expected by stakeholders to avoid full compliance with more expensive practices. Attention deflection can take three forms: first, companies can *substitute* a substantive CSR practice with a less rigorous one by developing voluntary self-regulation programmes and own-compliance rules to avoid standards that are more stringent. King and Lenox (2000) for instance studied the Responsible Care initiative that major players in the chemicals industry created to emphasize their CSR commitments. They argued that this standard was problematic because it was not only less demanding than governmental regulation, but also without sanction in case of breaches of the standard. Effective industry self-regulation, however, is difficult to maintain without explicit sanctions because participants have little incentive to invest the necessary resources to comply with the standard.

The second form of attention deflection is what Marquis and Toffel (2012) call *social image bolstering*. Here, business firms adopt some CSR practices to enhance their social or environmental reputation in order to deflect attention from other harmful or irresponsible activities. For instance, this happens if firms focus their CSR implementation on the easy-to-implement low-hanging fruits, without giving proper attention to those high-hanging fruits that might cause severe social or environmental damage but are costly to implement. In addition, several participants of the UNGC have been accused of bluewashing, because they use their affiliation with the 'blue' UN brand and the UNGC's principles to deflect attention from less responsible management practices (Berliner & Prakash, 2015).

Third, Marquis and Toffel (2012) identified *selective disclosure* as a strategy whereby companies conceal potentially negative aspects of their conduct by selectively revealing relatively benign CSR activities – something that comes close to what we discussed before as greenwashing. This happens if a firm disproportionally discloses positive information and benign CSR indicators to mislead consumers about actual performance and more harmful indicators while creating the false impression of transparency and compliance.

Decoupling can also have a spatial dimension, where responsible and irresponsible practices are geographically separated. Surroca and colleagues (2013) have shown that companies are creative in shifting irresponsible practices to subsidiaries or suppliers in developing countries. They show that to ensure compliance and maintain social legitimacy in the home country key markets, companies relocate activities to so-called pollution havens, that is, countries with lax regulation and stakeholder pressure. This applies specifically to less visible parts of a firm, namely subsidiaries that often are registered under a different name and thus make it more complicated for stakeholders to link the subsidiaries' activities to a well-known brand in their home country. Complex production networks and supply chains provide further opportunities to shift dirty businesses to pollution havens. Apple, for instance, makes a great effort to maintain its clean image in its key Western markets, while not actually producing any device itself. Rather, most production is outsourced to its key supplier Foxconn, which has repeatedly been in the media for systematic violation of labour rights.[52]

Wickert and colleagues (2016) offer a theoretical explanation of greenwashing specifically in large firms by looking at the organizational costs of CSR engagement. They argue that the mismatch between CSR 'walk' (i.e. substantive implementation) and 'talk' (i.e. symbolic impression management) is due to the large differential in costs for walk and talk, respectively. In large firms, the organizational costs for CSR talk are relatively low and decrease with increasing firm size due to economies of scale and scope. These costs include those associated with advertising, marketing, communication, reporting and disclosure of a firm's CSR activities. A sustainability report for example has to be produced only once and incurs fixed costs, and CSR attributes can be linked to a broader range of products, all of which make such talk relatively less expensive for a large firm. CSR walk, however, becomes increasingly costly as firm size increases. For large firms, substantively implementing CSR in practices and procedures throughout the value chain requires immense efforts and costly internal control mechanisms need to be established. As we discussed in the previous sections, companies are expected to reorganize their supply chains (e.g. stop sourcing from factories with low working standards or child labour), introduce cleaner product technologies or production processes (e.g. avoiding toxic substances, employing eco-efficient technologies), or spend resources on public policy issues (e.g. invest in education, healthcare or infrastructure). The 'large firm CSR implementation gap' is thus a form of greenwashing that can be attributed to internal organizational characteristics, because organizational costs make it less attractive for firms to focus on CSR walk, rather than talk.

Other studies have examined field-level dynamics that favour greenwashing. Delmas and colleagues (2013) studied CSR ratings and the rewards that stock markets provide based on those ratings. Interestingly, they found that markets grant higher rewards for the existence of CSR processes instead of CSR outcomes. This essentially favours greenwashing behaviour, because processes typically include only those CSR commitments, policies, management systems and participation in initiatives that often remain at a symbolic level without corresponding to substantive implementation. Investors, however, are less likely to reward outcome-based measures. Those measures include actual environmental impacts such as carbon dioxide emissions, levels of toxic releases, water usage, etc. Companies thus have a strong incentive for symbolic, but unsubstantiated, actions that are easy to communicate, convenient for environmental ratings and less costly to pursue, while there is little market-driven incentive to invest in expensive CSR-outcomes.

Scholars have also investigated reasons for greenwashing that can be attributed the behaviour of individual managers. Ormiston and Wong (2013), who studied the effects of CSR and CEO moral identity on CSiR, have conducted an insightful analysis. Examining the case of the oil company BP, the authors asked what the conditions are under which BP's socially responsible behaviour (e.g. an increased safety record) might have subsequently increased its less responsible behaviour (e.g. ignoring safety warnings) that ultimately contributed to the Deepwater Horizon oil spill in 2010. In essence, their study shows that prior CSR can be positively related to subsequent CSiR. This is because of what they call 'moral credits', which can be understood as accumulated ethical points which then allow the financing of unethical behaviour. They find that moral credits achieved through CSR engagement enable managers to engage in less-ethical stakeholder treatment or, in the case of BP, ignore important but costly safety measures, given that BP had already invested in other CSR activities elsewhere. In essence, their study shows that being ethical today does not necessarily imply being ethical tomorrow.

Overall, this research points to a range of social and environmental consequences of greenwashing. Next to the obvious ecological or social harm that is being covered and maintained by such impression management, it also contributes to the deterioration of consumer and investor trust in green brands. For instance, if a major player in an industry is caught cheating, such as Volkswagen in the Dieselgate scandal, the assumption that other players might commit similar forms of greenwashing is fairly warranted. Thus, the market for green products is damaged if the general level of trust in the reliability of such products decreases. Greenwashing also opens space for free-riders that, for instance, take advantage of fake labels and logos. Due to the complexity and sheer number of different logos commonly found on consumer products, people face severe difficulty in distinguishing reliable from unreliable logos, while the latter involve substantially lower costs for the companies that use them.

Greenwashing obviously can also have substantial negative effects on firms. Researchers have for instance examined the reputational effects of unsubstantiated and even hypocritical CSR behaviour. Yoon and colleagues (2006) analysed the relationship between consumer perceptions about CSR and a company's reputation. Their study confirms that CSR can indeed enhance reputation if these activities are perceived as sincere by consumers and backed by substantive action. However, they also show that CSR activities can be ineffective when the sincerity of motives is ambiguous. Moreover, reputation can be damaged if CSR activities are considered insincere or misleading, for instance when one of those seven sins of greenwashing is too easily detectable. Consumers might thus become suspicious as to whether the true motive behind a CSR activity is merely an empty facade and PR exercise, or whether it mirrors substantive efforts to become more socially and environmentally responsible in a firm's core business operations. Being caught greenwashing may thus also backfire and leave the company with a worse reputation than had it not talked about CSR at all.

While we have presented some important explanations for the prevalence of greenwashing in society, some research has also taken a somewhat more positive outlook and found that greenwashing might only be a temporary phenomenon that, due to certain triggers, turns into more substantive behaviour over time. Christensen and colleagues (2013) have developed the idea of 'aspirational talk' in CSR. They argue that greenwashing might reflect such aspirational talk, where announcing ideals and intentions, rather than reflecting actual behaviour (in this case, being socially responsible), may lead to the behaviour that actors have committed themselves to. Conceivably, managers who continually reflect on and speak about specific CSR activities and intentions in doing so commit themselves rhetorically to adopting them – in other words they 'talk into existence' the very CSR commitments that are made (Haack et al, 2012). Thus, they are more likely to align their acts with their words in order to avoid shame and embarrassment and not being seen as ceremonial props. A key condition, however, for such aspirational talk to materialize and not just remain a blunt lie is to have 'a public ceremony, with witnesses' (Taylor & Cooren, 1997: p. 422). In other words, constant monitoring and critical scrutiny of stakeholders, both internal ones such as employees and external ones such as NGOs, is important.

In this section, we have provided a snapshot of some of the most severe forms of greenwashing based on illustrative evidence. We have furthermore provided an array of theoretical accounts that explain the reasons why and under what conditions greenwashing is likely to occur. This, we hope, helps to better distinguish substantive from symbolic CSR engagement.

5 Looking Ahead: Setting the CSR Agenda for the Next Decade

The objectives of this section are:

- To provide an outlook of two key developments that will influence the CSR agenda of many business firms in the next decade, namely the question of 'digital responsibility' and how to contribute to the Sustainable Development Goals (SDGs).
- To suggest that due to ambiguous impacts of CSR actions, attention needs to shift from CSR *outputs* such as policy documents, to CSR *outcomes* such as real improvements in ecological and social conditions attributable to business activity.

In the previous sections, we discussed existing approaches to CSR and how many business firms practise it. We now turn to the question of what the CSR agenda for the next decade will most likely be. We will outline some emerging trends which we argue will become much more important and picked up by stakeholders and business firms as central CSR issues, and thereby further stretch the scope of what CSR entails and how it should be organized. First, we will discuss two important new developments that already impact the CSR agenda, both in research and practice. On the one hand, digitalization and the rise of big data-driven technologies pose an entirely new set of challenges for business firms. It remains to be determined what those new responsibilities are of companies that either supply or apply digital technologies. On the other hand, the SDGs have gained prominence as a set of universal targets to promote human development worldwide and explicitly call on the involvement of the private sector. Second, with regard to the ambiguous impacts of many CSR activities on actual social and environmental conditions, new forms of accountability are needed and a shift in understanding CSR not as a (never ending) 'journey' but as measuring its concrete outcomes and effects.

5.1 New Responsibilities in the Age of Digitalization

The importance of digital technologies for social and economic development and a growing focus on big data, algorithms and artificial intelligence (AI) have propelled internet companies into heated public and regulatory debates about their roles and responsibilities. Digital transformations are not only about innovation, social media and new possibilities for communication and collaboration, but also about profits, monopolies, surveillance and privacy and rights issues. For a long time, internet companies such as Google, Amazon and Facebook have been celebrated as drivers of growth, democratization and access to information. But we increasingly witness that such companies also seek to dominate commercial, technological, infrastructural, political and cultural spheres of society and to control as much information and data as possible.

Two of the major players, Google and Facebook, are repeatedly accused of gathering massive amounts of data without the explicit consent of their users, and thus become complicit in the abuse of such data,[53] for instance in connection with political campaigns. Moreover, the focus of societal concern is not only on those companies that develop and apply those technologies themselves, but also increasingly on traditional businesses, even family-owned firms that make use of digital technology and services to improve their core business. However, despite these challenges, we know surprisingly little about the

---

[53] http://time.com/5433499/tim-cook-apple-data-privacy/

resulting social responsibilities that internet companies themselves have or should have, and how other businesses relying on digital services and infrastructure interpret and develop their own 'digital responsibility' as part of their broader CSR agenda. Social responsibilities along 'digital supply chains' also remain a blind spot in the current CSR debate (see Flyverbom et al., 2019 for a summary). This includes the roles of providers and collectors, analysers and users of big data, and issues much beyond protection of personal data. While many internet companies have indeed addressed traditional CSR issues such as eco-efficiency and reduced energy usage for their servers, or provide a healthy work environment for their employees, a new set of responsibilities has emerged such as how to prevent hate speech and fake news. Researchers and practitioners have yet to find a consensus on how providers and users of social media and related technologies ought to deal with these new responsibilities.

Recent developments have also highlighted how the current approach of governments and business to the governance of the Internet and the adjacent technological space raises a host of ethical regulatory issues, as most of the new digital technologies operate within a massively unregulated space. Examples include technological designs that facilitate the circulation of misinformation, governments filtering or turning off the Internet at will, and states and corporations using digital traces to track and profile citizens and users. These developments raise crucial questions about the politics of data-driven processes, including de-anonymization and risks for privacy, forms of discrimination and abuse, trust, transparency and accountability. Cathy O'Neil's (2016) book, *Weapons of Math Destruction*, provides a critical account of how big data-driven business may pose a serious threat to equality, undermine democracy and consolidate discrimination. This is because 'algorithms and mathematical models create their own toxic feedback loops' (p. 11), and they contain many questionable assumptions that are 'camouflaged by math and go largely untested and unquestioned' (p. 7) by the broader public. In consequence, big data-driven technologies may lead to behaviour that systematically disadvantages certain groups of people, mostly from minorities, or they may facilitate the spread of false information that certain powerful groups may use for manipulation of public opinion.

We might witness the emergence of what could be called the 'digital industrial complex' which is characterized by vested interests of governments and major players in the digital economy that make up a political economy of the Internet (see also Flyverbom et al., 2019). This complex could, for instance, pose a serious threat to free and fair competition, as the very nature of most digital business models makes monopolies or at least oligopolies the only viable market structure. This underlines the market power that companies such as

Amazon and Google already have and how they might abuse it to the disadvantage not only of consumers but also of smaller firms. The scandal of Facebook and Cambridge Analytica, where around 50 million profiles of American internet users and their personal data had been misused (i.e. monetized) in the 2016 US presidential election, likewise might not have been incidental or simply a mistake, but rather systemic of Facebook's business model.[54] Some have even called tech companies the new 'robber barons' of the age of digitalization[55] that abuse their suppliers, employees and customers because of their market power, and do everything they can to defend this power and keep regulation at bay. What we see is that Internet and social media platforms increasingly have the character of a public good such as water supply, and calls have been made to dismantle monopolistic structures. Whether voluntary commitments, increased CSR and self-regulation will help to balance the opportunity of digital technologies to stimulate positive social change with the downsides that we have illustrated, or whether more hard regulation is necessary to harness its destructive potential, remains to be seen.

5.2 New Responsibilities Emerging from the Sustainable Development Goals

In September 2015, 193 member states of the UN reached a historic agreement by adopting a large-scale sustainable development agenda that encapsulates 17 broad goals aimed to end poverty, protect the planet and its people, and ensure more inclusive and equal living conditions around the globe (see Figure 6).[56] The 17 SDGs encompass 169 targets to be achieved by 2030, such as achieving gender equality and empowering women and girls, combating climate change and its implications, and revitalizing a global partnership for development that explicitly calls on the private sector to join forces with governments and civil society organizations in reaching these goals. One the one hand, it is argued that due to their increased size and reach, business firms contribute significantly to some of the world's most vital social and environmental problems, such as overfishing of the oceans, water scarcity, violation of human rights, corruption and deforestation. Business activity is at the heart of these (and other) problems. On the other hand, the call on business firms to join forces with governments and civil society reflects that they are also increasingly seen as part of the solution to many problems of a global nature.

---

[54] www.theguardian.com/technology/2018/mar/28/facebook-apple-tim-cook-zuckerberg-business -model?CMP=share_btn_link

[55] www.latimes.com/opinion/op-ed/la-oe-strauss-digital-robber-barons-break-up-monopolies -20160630-snap-story.html

[56] https://sustainabledevelopment.un.org/

Figure 6: The Sustainable Development Goals.

Source: United Nations; www.un.org/sustainabledevelopment/sustainable-development-goals/.

Indeed, several MNCs have already begun to address some of the SDGs and connected them to their CSR strategies. Unilever, for instance, the fast-moving, Dutch consumer goods multinational, has launched its 'Sustainable Living Plan' through which it makes a decisive effort to connect business objectives with several of the SDGs and in doing so aligns its CSR agenda with broad development goals. Corporations such as Unilever are increasingly seen as partners by governmental institutions and civil society actors that jointly mobilize resources in order to promote a common agenda.[57] While a few companies have taken a leadership position in taking a firm stance towards the SDGs, by their very nature, issues of such magnitude require coordinated and sustained effort from multiple and diverse stakeholders towards a clearly articulated problem or goal. George and colleagues (2016, p. 1881) therefore characterize the set of issues identified by the SDGs as a societal 'grand challenge', a 'specific critical barrier that, if removed, would help solve an important societal problem with a high likelihood of global impact through widespread implementation'. They further argue that achieving the SDGs would involve widespread changes in individual, organizational and societal behaviours, changes to how actions are organized and implemented, and progress in technologies and tools to solve these problems.

Business firms that make a commitment to implement the SDGs are challenged to clearly define which of these broad goals are relevant for their immediate business context and how to transform them into concrete action, practices and procedures. However, with the exception of a few leaders, many business firms still struggle to take a firm stance towards the SDGs, or they simply remain incomprehensible to most managers (Kolk et al., 2017). Nevertheless, many of them are directly relevant for companies, such as 'decent work and economic growth' (SDG 8), 'industry, innovation, and infrastructure' (SDG 9), and 'responsible consumption and production' (SDG 12). Other relevant SDGs include 'no poverty' (SDG 1), 'good health and well-being' (SDG 3), 'gender equality' (SDG 5) and 'reduced inequalities' (SDG 10). The challenge remains to achieve these clear targets through collective, collaborative and coordinated effort. More research into these questions is needed, but it is likely that the SDGs will become something of a new gold standard for CSR policies and strategies around the globe. At the same time, a critical stance might be needed because while corporate involvement can help to solve some of today's biggest problems, it may also create risk. For instance, it furthers the dependence on corporations as the dominant institution in modern life and as key providers of public welfare.

---

[57] www.unilever.com/sustainable-living/our-strategy/un-sustainable-development-goals/

5.3 New Forms of Accountability for CSR: From Outputs to Outcomes

In Section 4 we examined the problems related to measuring and accounting for concrete CSR impacts. Naturally, it is not the number of pages of the sustainability report that counts, but actual improvements in some clearly defined social and environmental conditions such as workplace accidents or carbon emissions. We argue that new forms of CSR accountability are therefore needed that imply a shift from looking at CSR *outputs* (i.e. CSR commitments, codes of conduct, CSR reports and policies, etc.) to considering concrete CSR *outcomes*. Such a turn to impact-oriented CSR would imply a fundamental shift in the dependent variables we look at, away from financial performance as a key variable towards some measure of sustainability performance as the main variable of concern.

Traditionally, scholars concerned with CSR have focused on the impact that CSR policies and activities have on *corporations*. This corporate-centric perspective on impact is particularly evident when looking into the rich literature that analyses the performance implications of CSR (Wang et al., 2016; Orlitzky et al., 2003). While this literature tells us a lot about the ways in which CSR policies can impact corporate financial and non-financial performance, we know surprisingly little about whether and in what ways CSR activities create outcomes that profit final beneficiaries other than shareholders, such as workers, smallholders in global supply chains, the natural environment and society more generally (Margolis & Walsh, 2003). Although work on corporate social performance (Wood, 1991) has emphasized the need to study CSR-related impacts, the focus is often on *outputs* (e.g. commitments made to CSR; the production of CSR reports; data collected on CSR indicators; the existence of CSR policies/ programmes; membership in various CSR initiatives). However, outputs do not necessarily tell us much about the *outcomes* for final beneficiaries such as whether working conditions have actually been improved. In fact, it is possible that corporations produce superb CSR outputs without producing many CSR outcomes, and in doing so disguise their true impact on society (Wickert et al., 2016).

This may suggest that research has been overly concerned with examining how corporations should design their CSR activities to benefit primarily themselves, while overlooking the important question of whether these outputs actually lead to substantial outcomes that are beneficial to those targeted by the various CSR activities. The question that stands out is how social responsibilities can be organized in order to create outcomes that are beneficial for society and the natural environment, and are not restricted to outputs that primarily improve the financial performance of shareholders.

Focusing on outcomes would, for instance, also include an issue that has as yet been largely under the radar of public attention and scrutiny, but is gaining more salience in the media and in academic research (e.g. Dowling, 2014; Muller & Kolk, 2015). Namely, corporate tax evasion and avoidance strategies are alerting not only the broader public but also politicians around the world. Tech companies such as Amazon are repeatedly in the media and accused of massive tax avoidance. A report by *The Guardian*[58] for instance headlined that 'Amazon made an $11.2bn profit in 2018 but paid no federal tax.' While the company's profits doubled in 2018, instead of paying the statutory 21 per cent income tax, a rate that 'less clever' SMEs are obliged to pay to finance a functioning government, Amazon even reported a US$129m income tax rebate, leading to a tax rate of -1 per cent. Such practices are increasingly considered unethical by societal stakeholders. Thus, the notion of corporate tax responsibility, and the actual and fair share of tax contributions that MNCs in particular make will most likely be more prominent in future discussions about CSR-related outcomes.

Furthermore, focusing on CSR outcomes calls for research that discusses the methodological conundrums surrounding impact-related work. For instance, it is often difficult to adequately isolate the impact of CSR activities on final beneficiaries, such as when asking the following question: is a worker better off because of a firm's CSR activities, or would the improvements have occurred without any CSR-related engagement? Research should examine new techniques for measuring the impact of CSR, especially related to questions of assessing intangible and largely abstract outcomes (e.g. the beauty of nature, or the socio-cultural fabric that holds a society together). Corresponding research questions include: how to attribute CSR outputs to tangible and intangible social and environmental outcomes? How to link an organization's CSR outputs to its CSR outcomes? How to measure the effectiveness of CSR outputs with regard to outcomes for various final beneficiaries?

If CSR-related outcomes are studied, they are often discussed in isolation, such as when looking at whether workers benefit from ethical trade. Such a perspective neglects that trade-offs between different outcomes can exist in some areas. Positive outcomes for some final beneficiaries can be negative outcomes for others. Also, reaching some outcomes may produce positive/ negative unintended consequences on other outcome-related measures, such as when increased water availability can have positive effects on food security. Thus, a question for research to ask is how trade-offs between different positive

---

[58] www.theguardian.com/technology/2019/feb/15/amazon-tax-bill-2018-no-taxes-despite-billions-profit

and negative social and environmental outcomes can be balanced. A related question is how to assess the overall weighted impact of CSR outcomes considering both negative and positive outcomes for final beneficiaries?

Lastly, there is still a dearth of research that provides meaningful indicators that reflect socially and environmentally desirable outcome dimensions instead of narrow measures of output with a limited list of beneficiaries. Here, a promising new research agenda emerges at the intersection of accountability studies that have long been concerned with social and environmental accounting, and organizational research that asks how to organize for such outcomes. The corresponding research questions include: how to devise accountability structures that adequately capture both CSR outcomes and outputs for final beneficiaries? What types of accountability can we distinguish when researching CSR outcomes?

Looking at CSR outcomes rather than outputs would also imply no longer seeing CSR as a 'journey', as many business firms commonly phrase it. Journeys, it appears, often lead to nowhere, have vague and ambiguous targets, and as long as the journey is lasting accountability is difficult because one is still 'in progress' to somewhere. The SDGs are important in this regard because they provide a clearly defined and objectively measurable set of desired outcomes. What remains a challenge for researchers and managers alike is to find ways to reach those objectives.

References

Banerjee, B. (2008). Corporate social responsibility: the good, the bad and the ugly. *Critical Sociology*, 34, 51–79.

Bansal, P., & Song, H.-C. (2017). Similar but not the same: Differentiating corporate responsibility from sustainability. *Academy of Management Annals*, 11, 105–49.

Barnett, M. L. (2007). Stakeholder influence capacity and the variability of financial returns to corporate social responsibility. *Academy of Management Review*, 32, 794–816.

Barney, J. B. (1991). Firm resources and sustained competitive advantage. *Journal of Management*, 17, 99–120.

Baumann-Pauly, D., Wickert, C., Spence, L., & Scherer, A. G. (2013). Organizing corporate social responsibility in small and large firms: Size matters. *Journal of Business Ethics*, 115(4), 693–705.

Berliner, D., & Prakash, A. (2015). 'Bluewashing' the firm? Voluntary regulations, program design, and member compliance with the United Nations Global Compact. *Policy Studies Journal*, 43(1), 115–38.

Berrone, P., Cruz, C., Gomez-Mejia, L., & Larraza-Kintana, M. (2010). Socioemotional wealth and corporate responses to institutional pressures: Do family-controlled firms pollute less? *Administrative Science Quarterly*, 55, 82–113.

Bitaraf, K. (2015). The evolution of CSR drivers. *Unpublished working paper.* Amsterdam: Vrije Universiteit.

Bondy, K., Moon, J., & Matten, D. (2012). An institution of corporate social responsibility (CSR) in multinational corporations (MNCs): Form and implications. *Journal of Business Ethics*, 111, 281–99.

Bowen, H. R. (1953). *Social Responsibilities of the Businessman*. New York: Harper & Row.

Bowen, F. (2014). *After Greenwashing: Symbolic Corporate Environmentalism and Society*. Cambridge: Cambridge University Press.

Brammer, S., & Millington, A. (2008). Does it pay to be different? An analysis of the relationship between corporate social and financial performance. *Strategic Management Journal*, 29, 1325–43.

Bromley, P., & Powell, W. W. (2012). From smoke and mirrors to walking the talk: Decoupling in the contemporary world. *Academy of Management Annals*, 6(1), 483–530.

Campbell, J. L. (2007). Why would corporations behave in socially responsible ways? An institutional theory of corporate social responsibility. *Academy of Management Review*, 32, 946–67.

Carroll, A. B. (1991). The pyramid of corporate social responsibility: Toward the moral management of organizational stakeholders. *Business Horizons*, 34(4), 39–48.

Christensen, L., Morsing, M., & Thyssen, O. (2013). CSR as aspirational talk. *Organization*, 20, 372–93.

Christmann, P., & Taylor, G. (2006). Firm self-regulation through international certifiable standards: Determinants of symbolic versus substantive implementation. *Journal of International Business Studies*, 37, 863–78.

Crane, A. (2013). Modern slavery as a management practice: Exploring the conditions and capabilities for human exploitation. *Academy of Management Review*, 38(1), 49–69.

Crane, A., & Matten, D. (2015). *Business Ethics*. Oxford: Oxford University Press.

Crane, A., Palazzo, G., Spence, L., & Matten, D. (2014). Contesting the value of 'Creating Shared Value'. *California Management Review*, 56, 130–53.

Delmas, M. & Burbano, V. (2011). The drivers of greenwashing. *California Management Review*, 54, 64–87.

Delmas, M., Etzion, D., & Nairn-Birch, N. (2013). Triangulating environmental performance: what do corporate social responsibility ratings really capture? *Academy of Management Perspectives*, 27, 255–67.

Devinney, T. M. (2009). Is the socially responsible corporation a myth? The good, the bad, and the ugly of corporate social responsibility. *Academy of Management Perspectives*, 23, 44–56.

DiMaggio, P. J., & Powell, W. W. (1983). The iron cage revisited: Institutional isomorphism and collective rationality in organizational fields. *American Sociological Review*, 48(2), 147–60.

Donaldson, T., & Preston, L. E. (1995). The stakeholder theory of the corporation: Concepts, evidence, and implications. *Academy of Management Review*, 20, 65–91.

Dowell, G., & Muthulingam, S. (2017). Will firms go green if it pays? The impact of disruption, cost, and external factors on the adoption of environmental initiatives. *Strategic Management Journal*, 38, 1287–304.

Dowling, G. R. (2014). The curious case of corporate tax avoidance: Is it socially irresponsible? *Journal of Business Ethics*, 124, 173–84.

Flammer, C. (2013). Corporate social responsibility and shareholder reaction: The environmental awareness of investors. *Academy of Management Journal*, 56, 758–81.

Fleming, P., & Jones, B. (2013). *The End of Corporate Social Responsibility: Crisis and Critique*. London: SAGE.

Flyverbom, M., Deibert, R., & Matten, D. (2019). The governance of digital technology, big data, and the internet: New roles and responsibilities for business. *Business & Society*, 58, 3–19.

Freeman, R. E. (1984). *Strategic Management: A Stakeholder Approach*. Boston: Pitman.

Freeman, R. E., Harrison, JS., & Zyglidopoulos, S. (2018). *Stakeholder Theory: Concepts and Strategies*. Cambridge: Cambridge University Press.

Friedman, M. (1970). The social responsibility of business is to increase its profits. *New York Times Magazine*, September 13.

George, G., Howard-Grenville, J., Joshi, A., & Tihanyi, L. (2016). Understanding and tackling societal grand challenges through management research. *Academy of Management Journal*, 59, 1880–95.

Global Witness (2017). *Time to Dig Deeper*. August 2017. London, UK.

Haack, P., Schoeneborn, D., & Wickert, C. M. J. (2012). Talking the talk, moral entrapment, creeping commitment? Exploring narrative dynamics in corporate responsibility standardization. *Organization Studies*, 33(5–6), 815–45.

Habermas, J. (2001). *The Postnational Constellation: Political Essays*. Cambridge, UK: Polity Press.

Halme, M., Rintamäki, J., Knudsen, JS., Lankoski, L., & Kuisma, M. (2018). When is there a sustainability case for CSR? Pathways to environmental and social performance improvements. *Business & Society*, 1–47. https://doi.org/10.1177/0007650318755648

Hawn O., & Ioannou I. (2016). Mind the gap: The interplay between external and internal actions in the case of corporate social responsibility. *Strategic Management Journal*, 37(13), 2569–88.

Hemingway, C. A., & Maclagan, P. W. (2004). Managers' personal values as drivers of corporate social responsibility. *Journal of Business Ethics*, 50(1), 33–44.

Jensen, M. C. (2002). Value maximization, stakeholder theory, and the corporate objective function. *Business Ethics Quarterly*, 12(2), 235–56.

Jones, T. M. (1995). Instrumental stakeholder theory: A synthesis of ethics and economics. *Academy of Management Review*, 20, 404–37.

Karpoff, J. M. (2014). The grey areas of firm behaviour: an economic perspective. *Socio-Economic Review*, 12, 167–76.

Kim, Y. H., & Davis, G. F. (2016). Challenges for global supply chain sustainability: Evidence from conflict minerals reports. *Academy of Management Journal*, 59(6), 1896–916.

King, A. A., & Lenox, M. J. (2000). Industry self-regulation without sanctions: the chemical industry's responsible care program. *Academy of Management Journal*, 43(4), 698–716.

Kolk, A., Kourula, A., & Pisani, N. (2017). Multinational enterprises and the Sustainable Development Goals: what do we know and how to proceed? *Transnational Corporations*, 24(3), 9–32.

Kourula, A., Moon, J., Salles-Djelic, M. L., & Wickert, C. (2019). New roles of government in the governance of business conduct: Implications for management and organizational research. *Organization Studies*, forthcoming.

Lester, S. E., Costello C., Rassweiler A., Gaines, S. D., & Deacon, R. (2013). Encourage sustainability by giving credit for marine protected areas in seafood certification. *PLoS Biology* 11(12), e1001730.

Lyon, T. P., & Maxwell, J. W. (2011). Greenwash: Environmental disclosure under threat of audit. *Journal of Economics and Management Strategy*, 20(1), 3–41.

Lyon, T., & Montgomery, A. (2015). The means and end of greenwash. *Organization & Environment*, 28, 223–49.

Margolis, J. D., & Walsh, J. P. (2003). Misery loves companies: Rethinking social initiatives by business. *Administrative Science Quarterly*, 48, 268–305.

Marquis, C., & Toffel, M. (2012). When do firms greenwash? Corporate visibility, civil society scrutiny, and environmental disclosure. Working Paper: Harvard Business School.

Marquis, C., & Qian, C. (2014). Corporate social responsibility reporting in China: Symbol or substance? *Organization Science*, 25(1), 127–48.

Marquis, C., & Tilcsik, A. (2016) Institutional equivalence: How industry and community peers influence corporate philanthropy. *Organization Science* 27(5), 1325–41.

Marquis, C., Toffel, M., & Zhou, Y. (2016). Scrutiny, norms, and selective disclosure: A global study of greenwashing. *Organization Science*, 27(2), 483–504.

Matten, D., & Crane, A. (2005). Corporate citizenship: Toward an extended theoretical conceptualization. *Academy of Management Review*, 30(1), 166–79.

Matten, D., & Moon, J. (2008). 'Implicit' and 'explicit' CSR: A conceptual framework for a comparative understanding of corporate social responsibility. *Academy of Management Review*, 33(2), 404–24.

McWilliams, A., & Siegel, D. (2001). Corporate social responsibility: A theory of the firm perspective. *Academy of Management Review*, 26, 117–27.

Meyer, J., & Rowan, B. (1977). Institutionalized organizations: Formal structure as myth and ceremony. *American Journal of Sociology*, 83, 340–63.

Mitchell, R. K., Agle, B. R., & Wood, D. J. (1997). Toward a theory of stakeholder identification and salience: Defining the principle of who and what really counts. *Academy of Management Review*, 22, 853–86.

Muller, A., & Kolk, A. (2015). Responsible Tax as Corporate Social Responsibility: The Case of Multinational Enterprises and Effective Tax in India. *Business & Society*, 54, 435–63.

O'Neil, C. (2016). *Weapons of Math Destruction*. Largo: Crown Books.

Orlitzky M., Schmidt F. L., & Rynes, S. L. (2003). Corporate social and financial performance: A meta-analysis. *Organization Studies*, 24(3), 403–41.

Ormiston, M. E., & Wong, E. M. (2013). License to ill: The effects of corporate social responsibility and CEO moral identity on corporate social irresponsibility. *Personnel Psychology*, 66, 861–93.

Paine, L. S. (1994). Managing for organizational integrity. *Harvard Business Review*, 1994, 72(2), 106–17.

Palazzo, G., & Richter, U. (2005). CSR business as usual? The case of the tobacco industry. *Journal of Business Ethics*, 61, 387–401.

Porter, M. E., & Kramer, M. R. (2006). Strategy and society: The link between competitive advantage and corporate social responsibility. *Harvard Business Review*, 84(12), 78–92.

Porter, M. E., & Kramer, M. R. (2011). The big idea: Creating shared value. *Harvard Business Review*, 89(1–2), 62–67.

Reinecke, J., & Ansari, S. (2016). Taming wicked problems: The role of framing in the construction of corporate social responsibility. *Journal of Management Studies*, 53, 299–329.

Risi, D. (2013). Compliance and its effectiveness in preventing unethical behavior: Analysis of the Siemens Business Conduct Guidelines. In Sandra Brändli, Roman Schister, & Aurelia Tamò (eds.): *Multinationale Unternehmen und Institutionen im Wandel - Herausforderungen für Wirtschaft, Recht und Gesellschaft*. Bern: Stämpfli, 291-310.

Risi, D. (2016). Longitudinal comparison between CSR implementation and CSR function's resource access. *Academy of Management Annual Meeting Proceedings*, 2016(1), 25–28, DOI:10.5465/AMBPP.2016.69.

Risi, D. (2018). Time and business sustainability: Socially responsible investing in Swiss banks and insurance companies. *Business & Society*, 1–31, DOI:10.1177/0007650318777721.

Risi, D., & Wickert, C. (2017). Reconsidering the 'symmetry' between institutionalization and professionalization: The case of corporate social responsibility managers. *Journal of Management Studies*, 54(5), 613–46.

Scherer, A. G., & Palazzo, G. (2007). Toward a political conception of corporate responsibility: Business and society seen from a Habermasian perspective. *Academy of Management Review*, 32(4), 1096–120.

Scherer, A. G., & Palazzo, G. (2011). The new political role of business in a globalized world: A review of a new perspective on CSR and its implications for the firm, governance, and democracy. *Journal of Management Studies*, 48(4), 899–931.

Schrempf, J. (2014). A social connection approach to corporate responsibility: The case of the fast-food industry and obesity. *Business & Society*, 53(2), 300–32.

Scott, W. R. (2008). Approaching adulthood: The maturing of institutional theory. *Theory and Society*, 37, 427–42.

Shabana, K. M., Buchholtz, A. K., & Carroll, A. B. (2017). The institutionalization of corporate social responsibility reporting. *Business & Society*, 56(8), 1107–35.

Sharma, S., & Henriques, I. (2005). Stakeholder influence on sustainability practices in the Canadian forest products industry. *Strategic Management Journal*, 26(2), 159–80.

Strand, R. (2013). The chief officer of corporate social responsibility: A study of its presence in top management teams. *Journal for Business Ethics*, 112(4), 721–34.

Surroca, J., Tribó, J. A., & Zahra, S. (2013). Stakeholder pressure on MNEs and the transfer of socially irresponsible practices to subsidiaries. *Academy of Management Journal*, 56, 549–72.

Tashman, P., Marano, V., & Kostova, T. (2019). Walking the walk or talking the talk? Corporate social responsibility decoupling in emerging market multinationals. *Journal of International Business Studies*, 50(2), 153–71.

Taylor, J. R., & Cooren, F. (1997). What makes communication 'organizational'? How the many voices of a collectivity become the one voice of an organization. *Journal of Pragmatics* 27: 409–38.

Vogel, D. J. (2005). Is there a market for virtue? The business case for corporate social responsibility. *California Management Review*, 47(4), 19–45.

Vishwanathan, P., van Oosterhout, H. J., Heugens, P.P.M.A.R., Duran, P., & van Essen, M. (2019). Strategic CSR: a concept building meta-analysis. *Journal of Management Studies*.

Waddock, S. (2008). Building a new institutional infrastructure for corporate responsibility. *Academy of Management Perspectives*, 22, 87–108.

Wang, Q., Dou, J., & Jia, S. (2016). A meta-analytic review of corporate social responsibility and corporate financial performance: The moderating effect of contextual factors. *Business & Society*, 55(8), 1083–121.

Wickert, C. (2016). Managing 'political' corporate social responsibility in small- and medium-sized enterprises: A conceptual framework. *Business & Society*, 55(6), 792–824.

Wickert, C., Scherer, A. G., & Spence, L. J. (2016). Walking and talking corporate social responsibility: Implications of firm size and organizational cost. *Journal of Management Studies*, 53, 1169–96.

Wickert, C., & de Bakker, F. G. A. (2018). Pitching for social change: Towards a relational approach to selling and buying social issues. *Academy of Management Discoveries*, 4(1), 1–24.

Windsor, D. (2006). Corporate social responsibility: Three key approaches. *Journal of Management Studies*, 43(1), 93–114.

Wood, D. J. (1991). Corporate social performance revisited. *Academy of Management Review*, 16, 691–718.

Yoon, Y., Gürhan-Canli, Z., & Schwarz, N. (2006). The effect of corporate social responsibility (CSR) activities on companies with bad reputations. *Journal of Consumer Psychology*, 16, 377–90.

Young, I. (2004). Responsibility and global labor justice. *Journal of Political Philosophy*, 12(4), 365–88.

Zadek, S. (2004). The path to corporate responsibility. *Harvard Business Review*, 82(12), 125–32.

Business Strategy

J.-C. Spender
Rutgers Business School

J.-C. Spender is a visiting scholar at Rutgers Business School and a research professor at Kozminski University. He has been active in the business strategy field since 1971 and is the author or co-author of seven books and numerous papers. His principal academic interest is in knowledge-based theories of the private sector firm and their management.

Advisory Board

About the Series

Business strategy's reach is vast, and important too since wherever there is business activity there is strategizing. As a field, business strategy has a long history – from medieval and colonial times to today's developed and developing economies. This series offers a place for interesting and illuminating research, including industry and corporate studies, strategizing in service industries, in the arts, the public sector and in the new forms of internet-based commerce. It also covers today's expanding gamut of analytical techniques.

Cambridge Elements ≡

Business Strategy

Printed in the United States
By Bookmasters